College Is Yours
2.0

Preparing, Applying and Paying
for Colleges
Perfect for You

by Patrick O'Connor, Ph.D.

Outskirts Press, Inc.
Denver, Colorado

College is Yours 2.0
Preparing, Applying and Paying for Colleges Perfect for You

Patrick J. O'Connor, Ph.D.

Outskirts Press, Inc.
10940 South Parker Road- 515
Parker, Colorado 80134
888/OP-BOOKS

www.outskirtspress.com
info@outskirtspress.com

www.collegeisyours.com
collegeisyours@comcast.net

Cover and interior design: Bonnie Schemm
Cover photo: iStockPhoto.com. *All rights reserved. Used with permission.*
Author photo, back cover: Michelle Stamler, The Roeper School.
All rights reserved. Used with permission.

V 2.0

Outskirts Press, Inc.
http://www.outskirtspress.com

ISBN: 978-1-4327-7807-1
LIBRARY OF CONGRESS: 2011912887

PRINTED IN THE UNITED STATES OF AMERICA

For my children,
whose clear vision and inner wisdom inspires.

For my wife,
who raised them by example.

Acknowledgments

To the parents and students at The Roeper School,
for the honor of watching their rich lives reach new heights each day.

To my colleagues throughout the globe,
for their tireless support of my students and my writing.

To Randall Dunn, for support of the *College is Yours* concept.

To Bonnie Schemm, for the book's design
and her continued counsel on all things graphic and good.

To Michelle Stamler, for the author's photo.

To Jeff Deutsch of *MichiganSEO.us*, Web designer extraordinaire,
for revamping *collegeisyours.com* to the next level.

To the Moms' Council — Susan Bruno, Lindsay Balmer Hinz, Lori Lutz,
Dianne O'Connor, Christie Peck and Kristan Sides White,
for all the suggestions for the updated book.

To Amy Voigt of Groves High School and Julie Gillikin of The Roeper School,
for help with the gerunds.

To Tina and everyone at Outskirts Press, who made the deadline work.

Table of Contents

Welcome. 8

Introductions. 10

1. The Big Picture and the Middle Road 12
2. The Key to Success 14
3. Two Kinds of Genuine Community Service. 16
4. Extra Curricular Activities 18
5. Summer Programs and "You've Been Nominated". 20
6. More Than a Checklist. 22
7. What Does a Good Mix of Extra Curriculars
   and Community Service Look Like?. 24
8. Tests to Take in 10th Grade 26
9. The Basics of Visiting a College 28
10. Highly Selective Colleges 30
11. Talking with your Parents about College 32
12. Working with Your Counselor 34
13. College Fairs 36
14. More Search Tools. 38
15. College Considerations for Fine and Performing Artists 40
16. College Considerations for Athletes 42
17. College Considerations for Students with Special Needs . . . 44
18. ACT and SAT 46
19. Test Prep. 48
20. Senior Schedule and More on College Visits 50
21. Making the List. 52
22. Safety Schools and Transferring 54
23. Is College Worth It?. 56
24. Have You Cleaned up your Facebook Page Yet? 59
25. Community Colleges and Grade Point Averages. 62
26. Application Deadlines 64
27. College Costs 66
28. The 20 Minute Meeting on Paying for College 68

29. The 20 Minute Meeting After That (College Costs, Part 3) . . 70
30. Letters of Recommendation — The Big Picture 72
31. Letters — The Nuts and Bolts 74
32. Applying Online and Using Common Applications. 76
33. The Biggest Hurdle is the First Application 78
34. Changing Your Schedule. 80
35. Lining Up an Interview. 82
36. ShowTime 84
37. Essays. 86
38. Essays, Part 2. 88
39. Essays, Part 3. 90
40. The Final Check 92
41. Second Guessing Your List? Guess Again. 94
42. Making it through Holiday Breaks without Being Broken. . . . 96
43. Scholarship Essays in 600 Words or Less 98
44. I Love You, You're Perfect — Now Go Study 100
45. A Word About Grade Grubbing: No 102
46. 20 Minute Meetings, To Be Continued 104
47. Understanding Financial Aid Awards 106
48. The Chapter to Read on March 15th 108
49. The Best Advice When a College Says No 110
50. Three Kinds of Decisions 112
51. Waitlists 114
52. Waiting for a Year 116
53. Still Can't Decide? Try This 118
54. The Final Exam of Choosing a College 120
55. What Really Got you In, and What Will Really Keep you Out . 122
56. Things to do Before College. 124
57. Once You're There 126
58. For Someday (I Hope Not) 128
59. What's Next. 130
60. 600 Words for Parents 133
    About the Author 135

Welcome

For too many families, choosing a college starts with a big fear — fear of college, fear of testing, fear of the future, fear of what you don't know. I don't know why that happens; when you were five and in kindergarten, you said, "The world is a big place," and that was pretty cool. Now that you're looking at college, you think, "The world is a big place," and it scares you to death. What changed?

To overcome this big fear, most families buy a big book — large, heavy, and a little intimidating in appearance. To most people, this makes sense — since picking a college is a big, weighty decision, you need a big, weighty book.

The truth is, choosing a college shouldn't start with a book — it should start with your heart. After 12 years in the learning business, you should have some ideas about yourself — who you are, what you like, the kinds of places you like to visit, the kinds of people you like to be with. By building your college choices on what you like, you're making sure every college you put on your list (and at the start, there can be as many as 20) has enough of the things you like to make it an OK place to study and to live. That last part can't be emphasized enough; this isn't just a place where you sit in a classroom and go home at 3 o'clock. This is your new home, even if you're not going to live on campus.

A few additional rules. First, you don't have to know what you're going to major in to pick a college. Yes, if music is a real passion, you'd be wise to apply to colleges that offer music — but most students pick a major that's offered by many colleges, and most students will change their majors at least twice in college. So majors can help, but if you don't have one, don't panic.

Second, you don't have to know what you're going to do with the rest of your life before you pick a college. This is *really* important, because while your friends will be cool with this, your parents, your girlfriend/boyfriend's parents, your neighbors, and your Aunt Henrietta may not be (see Chapter 42). Being able to pay your own light bill matters, so it does deserve some thought — but the hot jobs when college is over probably don't even exist now. If you have an idea, a dream, or the results of a career test, plug them into the college equation — but it's not the only part of the solution, and if it doesn't exist, it doesn't need to be a part at all right now.

Third, if you find you don't really know that much about yourself, don't open the book — every college will look good to you. Instead, try asking yourself these five questions:

1. What three things about my high school would I like to see at my college?

2. What three things about my high school do I never want to see again?

3. What three classes, clubs, or programs should my high school offer that it doesn't offer now?

4. What parts of my home town do I like and not like?

5. What three things would I like to do that I've never done before?

This isn't a comprehensive set of questions — just five to get you going. Once you have those questions answered, you're ready to open the book, or go online and do a college search. Size of school, location of school, campus life, major — you're ready to take on most of those questions now. And don't worry about cost just yet — we'll take that on in due time. For now, lead with your heart, your brain, and a little, weighty book.

The time to fear college is never. Enjoy.

Introductions

College admissions offices aren't perfect. Every year, students get admitted who end up dropping out, never coming, or getting grades that put them on the "Dean's List" nobody likes to talk about. On top of that, students get denied by colleges where they would have been great students, active leaders, and wealthy alumni donors. Either way, colleges hate to make mistakes, and they do the best they can — but the system isn't perfect.

Take admissions essays. Many colleges don't require essays; these colleges rely heavily on how you did on one test you took in your junior year of high school, which to me is just begging for trouble — but more on that later. Colleges that do ask for essays usually leave the topic up to you, because they want to hear about your life and what you think is important — as long as you don't use more than 500 or 600 words.

That's a bad vibe right off the jump. It seems like the colleges are convinced nothing could be so important in your life as to take up more than 500 words, and if you DARE use 501 words to talk about it — well, you're toast. It seems like they might as well say, "Tell us why you love your life, but be quick about it."

Not a perfect approach to building a meaningful relationship, right?

The thing is, there's another way to look at this. To begin with, admissions officers care about you very much. I have yet to meet a more compassionate, intelligent, thoughtful group of people.

Second, a 500 word essay doesn't always have a 500 word limit. We'll talk more about this later, but if you're telling a great story, many admissions officers would gladly read 550 words or so. I wouldn't push it much past 550, but I think you get the idea …

… which is this. Much of what you think about getting into college isn't quite right. Admissions officers aren't robots; essay limits aren't always absolute; test scores may not matter that much; college rankings are — hey, I'd better slow down. It's hard to say where all of these myths came from, but they're doing a lot of damage to students and families; I wrote this book to help turn that around.

Just a heads up before we get started. Just like college admissions, this book isn't perfect. I've tried to give you some general advice on the most important topics in selecting a college that's right for you, but putting the right blend of ideas together for individual needs and interests in one book is impossible. That's why there's *www. collegeisyours.com* where you can continue the discussion. Start by reading one or two chapters of the book each day, and really *think* about what the ideas mean to you. Once you're done with the whole book, look at the Web site, and keep the book handy through senior year — the chapters are designed to be easy to read.

Since we're in this together, I've limited my chapters to 600 words — just like some of your college essays. I'll want to say more, but I might bore some of you, and then you'd go looking for college help from the sources that made you nervous in the first place. Don't look back — you've got a future to build, and you need fresh, good information.

Ready?

P.S. That part about the 500 word essay really being a 550 word essay? That won't work at Yale. There, if you get to 501, you really are toast.

Chapter 1

THE BIG PICTURE AND THE MIDDLE ROAD

Your parents will tell you applying to college was easy when they were young. According to them, they got up early one Saturday morning, took a test they'd never heard of, applied to one or two colleges their friends applied to, got in to at least one of them, and that was it. Simple.

Fast forward to today. Your friends are freaking about college, the home page of your computer is a "vocabulary question of the day" Web site, and even your parents — the ones who tell you how easy it was for them to apply to college — made you volunteer at a soup kitchen at age six, since that "looks good" to a college. With all of that going on, it's hard to believe a college choice could be simple — after all, even the college rankings say it's hard.

To those of you who hope your choice is as easy as your parents', and to those of you who are test-prepped up to here, let me offer another choice:

Live a rich, full life today, and apply only to colleges you love.

Colleges want students who get up every day and live, who go to high schools with limited choices and blaze new trails in learning that turn teachers' heads, or go to fancy high schools and squeeze every drop of learning out of every challenging class. They want students who have seen a problem down the block and implement a powerful solution, and they want students who flew half way across the world and gave of their hands, hearts and minds to people they will never see again. They want students who will push the status quo and lead the culture to new journeys, and they want students who celebrate the status quo by finding ways to make it better.

In other words, they want students who really *do*.

To those of you who have had test prep flash cards since birth, it might be time to retool a little. Colleges don't want students who just do the right things and say the right things and get the right scores. Sure, they take those kinds of students all the time, but they don't want to. Colleges will take students who let their lights shine over trained pigeons any day, except the real doers are few and far between — and if you think they can't tell the difference, you are vastly underestimating the intelligence of these folks.

At the same time, those of you who are hoping college selection will be a cakewalk need to ramp it up a gear or two. It could be the college you're dreaming of is just the place for you, but if the best reason you can give for going to that school is "Why not?", it's time you introduced yourself to your passion and purpose for learning. It not only makes each day a little brighter, it improves you chances of finishing college once you start.

It would be easy to believe that the key to college is training; that would give you a reason to be so busy with so much essay coaching and such that you wouldn't have time to think about what you're doing. It would also be easy to believe that your dream school will meet your needs — unless you haven't been awake enough to know what your needs really are. Like most of life, there's a better middle road to take if your destination is college — and your navigation system starts on the next page.

Chapter 2
THE KEY TO SUCCESS

Ninth graders are either reading this book because they're overly cranked up about college, or because they can't leave the house until they finish. Read the next six chapters, then tell the folks I said to come back next year.

The most important thing every college cares about is grades. Unless we're talking art or music school, your admission to a college most depends on getting great grades in challenging classes — not just in 11th grade, not once you're in college, but starting now. Not everyone can do this all of the time — in fact, very few people can — but the closer you get to this level, the more choices you have, and the college selection process is all about having choices.

So how do you get good grades? Be a good student.

I know, I know — that's *some* counseling, right? But most people don't go through high school as students — they go as guests, waiting for the teachers to tell them to do something. Once asked, they do homework, pass tests, write papers, get OK grades — but they never put their heart into it, or really think about what they're doing. No wonder students are a wreck when they fill out college applications; they've spent three years doing things that never really made sense to them, and when colleges ask them to write about the most important things they've learned as a student, they don't know what to say.

It's time to stop the stress and the guessing, even though your friends may be college bound thanks to that terrible twosome. If your math teacher assigns 15 problems, do those, and the next three problems after that; then read the math book (yeah — *read* the math book) to make sure what you learned today makes sense with what you learned yesterday. If your English teacher assigns 15 pages of reading, take notes on the reading as you go; this will require reading, stopping, thinking, and writing, and you can already do all of those things. Add to these notes every night, and imagine the teacher's surprise next week when someone actually answers the question, "How does all of this tie together?"

If these last two ideas scare you, you might want to sit down. When your history teacher asks for a 250 word paper, write 400 or 500 — in your own words — after you've compared the information in your textbook with what you learned from two credible history Web sites (and as you write, don't forget that reading, stopping, thinking, and writing thing). When you type the essay, put the words "ROUGH DRAFT" in big letters on the top page. Three days before the paper's due, ask your teacher to look it over with you before school; take notes during your meeting, and use those when you write the final draft, which is turned in on time.

These three things alone might not improve your grades, but you get the idea. Colleges like students who care about learning, and who are good at learning; if you push yourself and go the extra mile, you'll soon be better at both (even if you're currently getting As just on natural ability). This might require some changes in your social schedule (there are always study groups!), and you may have to speak with a teacher or two about study techniques (the study skills guru in your school probably teaches special education — really), but two or three months from now, you'll thank me — as a real student who knows who they are and loves to learn, and as a serious candidate for college.

Chapter 3

THE TWO KINDS OF GENUINE COPMMUNITY SERVICE

Good students give more to their studies, and good people make a better world. Colleges (and the rest of us) like to see both.

So here's Key Number 2 — go out now and be the good person you are, demonstrating that through community service and extra curricular activities.

Generally, there are two kinds of community service. The first is a regular, dedicated, volunteer effort to improve the conditions of your community that has no direct impact on your own life — in other words, you're making things better for others more than you are for yourself. This would include things like volunteering at a soup kitchen, school, retirement home, tutoring program, a place of worship, the Red Cross — you get the idea. Volunteer work at a business would not count — that's more like an internship, externship, or job shadowing, which is important (see Chapter 4), but it isn't community service. Similarly, chores around your house don't count — they are also important, but that's more like, well, life.

"Required" volunteer work — community service or volunteer work you HAD to do to fulfill some kind of requirement (graduation requirement, Boy Scouts, being allowed to still live at home) is a little different, and a little confusing — you volunteered to do it because you had to? Still, it's improving the community, so it counts — but in fairness to the colleges you're applying to, you need to note that you completed this work as part of a requirement.

Regular, dedicated work means you're giving consistently. This generally means one to two hours a week, or for an intense period of time during the summer — starting in 9th grade. Remember, you're doing this because you want the world to be better, and are willing to do something about it; the wise people who review college applications can tell if you're doing this just to suck up to them, and that's very unflattering for everyone involved. If you're having trouble genuinely wanting to make a difference, go read the essays by Isabel Allende and Miles Goodwin in *This I Believe*, then come back when you're focused.

The second kind of community service is just as important, but less frequent. This is "roll up your sleeves" community service, where a brief and/or urgent need requires a concentrated period of time. Examples here include helping your local school put up new playground equipment for a day, boxing canned goods for a few hours to send to hurricane victims, spending a spring break with Habitat for Humanity, shoveling driveways of neighbors for free, and welcoming students at school orientation in the fall. Individually, these efforts are important, but small; combined, they are important and mighty. Colleges love to see this kind of community service, since it shows you are willing to pitch in on a moment's notice and make a difference — and we all know the power of small acts of kindness in both the lives of those you serve and in those who do the service.

Either way, community service only truly works if you are doing it out of a sense of love — for a neighbor, a stranger, or the world. College admissions officers have a way of peering into your heart that might be considered a little scary, except that it's good for us. It makes us keep the bigger picture in mind, that life isn't about glory or recognition — it's about living a rich, full life.

P.S. Mom and Dad, the best way to get the community service party started is as a family, even in 9th grade. Lead by example, and all that …

Chapter 4

EXTRACURRICULAR ACTIVITIES

Just like community service, extra curricular activities are important — but keep these key points in mind:

- Extra curriculars can be thought of as hobbies or interests — sports, clubs, summer classes, travel, work, jobs and internships are the big ones.

- You want a mix of extra curriculars. It's great to play sports for four years, or have the same job for a long time — but don't let one or two things be the only things on your list for all of high school. You're shooting for consistency *and* variety; if some of them show leadership on your part, that's a big plus.

- Not all extra curriculars exist at school. Since there are many activities offered at schools that you can't find in other places, you should try some of them — but look around your local community center, library, YMCA, or Boys and Girls' Club too.

- Extra curriculars and community service are two different things, but they can overlap. If your high school basketball team runs the elementary basketball league in the summer, you're doing both; the same with the French Club that visits retirement centers on a regular basis. Use your creative leadership skills — it makes for a great life and a unique item for a college app.

- It's more than OK to start a new club in your school or community. Filling a need also shows creativity and leadership — just do your best to include others, and create a solid foundation for the club to grow on *after* you're gone (selflessness rules in choosing a college!)

- Work hard, but keep balanced. If you're doing too much at once, your grades go down, you lose your focus, and nothing seems fun. If your team demands all of your time, back off on community service for a few months; if it's crunch time at work, you might have to pass up the Spanish Club this semester. There'll be enough time, provided you use enough wisdom to balance your studies, your community service, and your extra curriculars.

- Keep a log of all of the extra curricular activities as you try them. Waiting until senior year isn't the way to go — 9th grade will be hazy by then, and you want a clear list. Use a notebook (don't use a computer, because you might be using a different one come 12th grade), and have your parents and friends review the list, since they'll remember things you'll forget.

- Give yourself some credit. Your annual summer trip to Mexico may be a family reunion to you, but it's travel to a different country and culture to a college. And what if your reunion is in Georgia instead? It still puts you in a different place — put it down!

- At the same time, be clear and fair. There is a limit to making yourself sound good, and the limit is honesty. Detroit is about 10 minutes away from Canada, so my students sometimes tell colleges they are "international travelers." That's no way to build a relationship with a college. If you went to Canada, tell them that.

- Leave a page in your notebook for any awards or recognitions you may receive for school, community service, or extra curriculars. Colleges care about these, too, and they'll be easy to find if it's just a page away from your activities.

Your diet of extra curriculars should be like food at a good Super Bowl party — a great main course or two and interesting smaller appetizers. Do that, and you'll be ready for college, life, and some awesome tailgate parties.

Chapter 5

SUMMER PROGRAMS AND "YOU'VE BEEN NOMINATED"

Many students (and parents) spend a lot of time looking for the College Admissions X Factor, that extra class, program, or recognition that will, all by itself, guarantee any student admission at the college of their choice.

Some people believe this sure thing lies in the myriad summer programs colleges offer. From writing seminars to business camps to rock band mini-courses, these programs offer students an opportunity to follow a passion or try something new, focus on it for a week in the summer, and get a taste of what it's like to live on a college campus, on your own ...

... and those are the best (and only) three reasons to participate in these programs.

Colleges like to see students actively involved outside the classroom, and on-campus activities certainly fill that bill; but so does working all summer to build your college fund, reading through Ulysses all summer and hosting a blog for like-minded readers, and traveling to the Vietnam Memorial to help your mom honor the fallen soldiers she served with.

All these things can enrich your life and expand your world — and all of them (even summer programs) can be done mindlessly, with an MP3 player in your ear. Part of it is what you do, but a bigger part is what it does to you. Colleges will want to know both.

This is especially important if you're thinking that a summer program at an "elite college" will automatically offer you an admissions boost, especially at that college. Admissions representatives say your participation (even at programs their college doesn't host) will strengthen your application, but one program by itself isn't a sure bet to getting in. In some cases (that's some cases), a letter from a college professor teaching in the class can be a boost, but that letter is usually based on one week of interaction, so it has its limits, too.

It's great to want to do more, and summer programs are one way to do that — but only one way. Like high school, make the most of the program and learn as much as you can; that's the best guarantee the experience will be viewed favorably by colleges, but there is no magic wand.

Another source commonly thought to grease the admissions skids is the letters telling students they've been "nominated" to attend a summer program, join a select society, or have their name printed in a yearbook of other nominated students. These invitations almost always require some sort of membership fee; those that are free "invite" you to buy copies of the yearbook for you, your friends and neighbors, and the US Secretary of Education.

Some of these "by invitation" summer programs are good, but some aren't; all of them are usually quite expensive, and none of them are the sure thing you're looking for in admission to college. Ask around to see if other students have gone to them, and check with your counselor for more affordable activities, then proceed with care.

As for the societies and yearbooks, forget it. It's usually never clear who "nominated" you, and none of these programs are given any weight by most colleges, who tend to view them as money-making schemes. Some offers may tempt you with a scholarship — that's what they do with part of your "membership fee", and it's almost always won by someone else.

The pressure to get into the "right college" leads to a natural search for shortcuts and easy answers. But the pressure is a mirage, so you don't have to fix it. You just have to stay awake.

Chapter 6
MORE THAN A CHECKLIST

Since many colleges ask for lists — what sports you do, what clubs you've joined, what work you do in your community — some students develop a "checklist attitude" towards community service and extra curriculars. Instead of doing these things because they're great things to do, students see them as one more "thing", one more task to knock off to get into a great college. Then, just like 9th grade gym, once you're in, you're finished with that for good.

The truth is, it doesn't work that way. First, colleges can sort out the truly committed from the "list completers" in a heartbeat. The folks who are looking to beef up a college application join a dozen groups junior year, and give two hours total to each; the givers are active in a group or two starting in (or even before) ninth grade, contributing two to five hours a week to helping those in need, something they believe in. This kind of commitment usually leads to leadership opportunities, or chances to take a volunteer group in a new direction — but even if it doesn't, colleges will notice when a student gave 300 – 700 hours to a cause during high school, and still had time for studies, family, and a couple of extracurriculars.

Second, just like good study habits, these things improve your learning in a big way. Giving up your TV time or chat room time for the swim team, the chess club, and the homeless shelter puts you in the center of the real world, where you learn about the give and take of life, the differences between people, and the importance of everyone pitching in and doing their best. Colleges have a name for that kind of learning — they call it wisdom — and it is a highly valued commodity. By giving to the world outside of the classroom, you are showing an interest in the world, and a willingness to challenge yourself — what college wouldn't love to see that?

Third, doing these things now gets you ready for — hang on here — life after college. I know that's a few years and a zillion Friday nights down the road, but it's coming, and you need to be ready. If you can practice juggling school, service, and fun now, you'll be a Zen master at it by 25, and you'll stay with it until you're 125. Imagine a world where everybody knows how to work hard, give back, and let go. That would be like — like college forever!

It's usually right here where students say, "Yeah, but I stink at everything." Look — go to your town's health club this Saturday morning. The place won't be filled with athletic superstars, but with people who love to work out. Some will be ripped, some will be wearing trendy outfits, and some will be struggling to bench press 80 pounds — but they'll all be doing the best they can, trying to make a difference with what they've got, and loving the challenge they've made for themselves.

And that's the whole idea — love what you do so much that what the guy next to you thinks about you becomes irrelevant. Find a cause or two and some extra curriculars that mean something to you, and give your all. You might not get an award or a team captainship to throw on a college application — but then again you might. Either way, you'll have four solid years of taking a stand, of giving, living, and learning beyond the world of books — and that can make a huge difference, both to a college and to the world.

Chapter 7

WHAT DOES A GOOD MIX OF EXTRACURRICULARS AND COMMUNITY SERVICE LOOK LIKE?

Sara came home from a softball game last spring and was surprised to see her father's car in the driveway. May was a busy month in his line of work, so he usually went back to the office after watching Sara pitch, finished a little paperwork, and came home in time for a late dinner.

That day, he greeted his daughter in the kitchen. "Nice game, Ace!"

"Thanks, Daddy. Why are you home?"

He beamed at his 11th grade daughter and said, "I have a surprise. There's an overseas community service project heading to a small village in Haiti. They've opened a large orphanage there for children who lost parents in the earthquake, and they need volunteers to help with the babies, so the residents can rebuild their homes."

Sara peeled an orange while her father continued.

"You'd be there four days, and you'd be making a difference in the world. Your grades are strong and your pitching is great, but I think something like this could put you over the top at the colleges we're talking about. The Web site for the project is up on the computer. What do you say?"

Sara continued to peel the orange. "Can we talk about it at dinner?"

Her father was a little deflated, but he smiled back. "Sure, honey. I'm going to run back to the office for a little bit, but I'll see you at seven."

Dad came through the kitchen door at 7:15 and quickly took his place at the table with the rest of the family. After more congratulations for Sara's great game and a little razzing about her hair from her tech-savvy brother John, her dad said, "So, how about Haiti?"

Sara put her fork down slowly and looked up. "It's a great idea, Dad, but I looked on the Web site. Does this trip really cost $6,000?"

Her father choked on his ice water, while Sara's mom gave him a long, cold stare.

"We can afford this, Sara," he said, smiling faintly. "It's about your future."

Sara looked down at her placemat again, and swallowed hard. "Well, I looked up the name of the town I'd be going to. It turns out Habitat for Humanity is working there, too, and they need $4,000 for a new pump so the town can get fresh water again. I also called the Boys and Girls Club down on Wilson Street, and they said they could really use some help this summer.

"I sure appreciate the offer, Daddy, but don't you think it would be better if I stayed here, and we sent the $4,000 to Habitat for Humanity? That way, the town would have fresh water forever, John could get that new computer he'll need for high school next year, we'd have a little money left over for my college fund, and I could still make a difference in the world. It would just be a difference in my own neighborhood."

Sara's mother did a very bad job of trying to chew nonchalantly, while John tried hard to wipe the tears out of his eyes in a 14 year-old macho fashion. Her father's shoulders relaxed, as he smiled almost to himself, and said, "Yeah, honey. That's a great idea."

Sara is now a senior, waiting to hear from her colleges — but the question you should be asking yourself is not, "Where will she get in?"

The question to consider is, "Does it really matter?"

Chapter 8

TESTS TO TAKE IN 10TH GRADE

If there are any 9th graders here, let me gently recommend you put this book down and sign up for remedial math — you've had your six chapters, so your work here is finished for now.

In order to make a great college selection, 10th graders need to do four things. First, keep doing everything you started in 9th grade. Strong grades in challenging classes, frequent community service, and some solid extra curricular activities are the foundation of the House of College Knowledge, so keep cementing that foundation away. (Get it — Foundation? House? Cement? Boy — tough crowd!)

Second, it's time to build some windows in that house, and the first two involve four-letter words. (Oh, sure — now I have your attention.)

The PSAT gives juniors a peek at how the SAT works. Let me say that again — it's designed to give *juniors* a chance to see how the SAT works. The scores juniors earn on the PSAT may qualify them for scholarships through the National Merit Corporation. About 15 years ago, some 10th graders thought it might be a good idea to take the PSAT as sophomores — that way, they could get a feel for the test, then smoke it as juniors and grab some cash. This idea soon made sense to a lot of 10th graders, so now many schools offer the PSAT to 10th graders.

It's OK to take the PSAT in 10th grade, as long as you'll be OK with getting a less than perfect score. The PSAT measures Verbal Reasoning, Math and Writing, based on what the test writers think juniors should know — and you're a sophomore. Since there's a decent chance you haven't had everything that's on the test (and that's *really* true if you're not past Geometry or Algebra 2), your scores might not be what you think they should be. If you're cool with that, and you want to jump in and see what these tests are all about, go for it; if you think your chances at an Ivy League school will be trashed because your 10th grade PSAT could be low, let it go ...

… or try this. Your high school gets practice versions of the PSAT —
if you're taking the test, you'll get a copy when you sign up for the test
(use it to get ready!) If you're not taking the test, wait until the PSAT
has been given, then ask your counselor for any leftover practice tests.
Take it home, time yourself, then check your answers. It's free, it's
simple to do, and nobody gets hurt.

Whether you do PSAT or not, 10th graders should take the PLAN.
PLAN is a preliminary ACT, and ACT is the other test many colleges
use as part of the admission process. PLAN is designed to be given in
10th grade, so the results you get will give you an honest picture of how
well you know the stuff you've been studying. There's a practice test
here, too — it's just that not as many high schools give PLAN. If yours
does, go for it. Finally, if tests just take too much out of you, you may
qualify for extra time or other accommodations to take PLAN or PSAT
— ask your school now.

Some people spazz about tests, because they see them as windows
into their minds or souls. Taking PLAN and PSAT as 10th graders is
really a one way window, since you get to peek at what colleges expect
you to know, but colleges will never ask to see your scores. This is too
good to pass up — make your move!

Chapter 9

THE BASICS OF VISITING A COLLEGE

High school athletes watch the pros to get tips and get inspired. High school artists visit museums to see classic art, so they can create new art. High school writers read the works that made new inroads, so they are psyched to forge new paths.

And that's why 10th graders visit college campuses.

Hanging out on a college campus can give you a natural buzz, a sense that something's going on here, that maybe this place can help you make some dreams come true. That's where you want to be — that's the attitude that will get you into a college that's right for you, and help you make sense out of high school.

So the third thing you do as a 10th grader is take a road trip (with your parents, if possible).

There are lots of ways to visit a college, but here are some ideas:

- Start local. You can learn a lot by visiting any college campus, even if you're not sure you'd really go there. With any luck, the first thing you'll learn is that every college has lots of fast food places, 24-hour stores, and cool places to buy sweatshirts. Beyond that, you need to figure out what makes a college special to you — a particular major, class size, the way the profs treat the students — and the college across the street can help you sort some of that out as well as a college across the country.

- Take a tour, and fill out the registration card (this is important — trust me). College admissions offices usually host campus tours — call them two weeks ahead of time and sign up. Remember, the tour is their chance to show what they think are the best parts of the college — and that can say a lot. If a tour guide doesn't really answer your questions (ask a lot), or if you get the feeling the college isn't very interesting, this might not be the place for you.

- Customize your visit. When you call about the tour, ask to sit in on classes (that's right — you DON'T visit a college on a day when there are no classes), or to talk with a prof in the department you're interested in. If you care about something special — the workout areas, the research labs, the library — ask to see it. Ask to see a dorm; some colleges won't show them to you, but ask anyway. Try the food; it may not be like home, but it's a great way to find out what the other students are like, and that is HUGE. You can also go to the big game — just be sure to see some classes in action.

- Compare colleges. As you visit each college, write down your impressions right after the visit is over. This may seem a little geeky, but since you'll be visiting lots of campuses over a few years, it's the best way to remember what you saw, and to sort out colleges you like from those you don't.

If you do a campus visit the right way, you'll learn a lot about college, and even more about yourself. Both of these things can inspire the learning you're doing in high school and the life you're living right now. We have a name for that in college counseling — it's called a deal. Take it.

P.S. Whether you get to a campus or not, read *Colleges That Change Lives* by Lauren Pope. It's not quite a campus visit, but it will point you in the right direction about the purpose of college in general.

Chapter 10
HIGHLY SELECTIVE COLLEGES

With some college visits behind you and the wisdom of Lauren Pope in you (I'm telling you, read that book), you might be thinking serious college thoughts. You know who you are, you know what you want, you're past what others think about you, and you've learned how to work hard.

Maybe it's time to think about a highly selective college.

First, an explanation. A highly selective college (at least my definition) is a college that admits about 15% or less of everyone who applies there. The number of these colleges has gone up, and their admit rates have gone down — some to as low as 3.5%. For confused folks, these numbers lead them to apply ("I might be one of the lucky 11%!") or not apply ("Man, nobody applies there anymore — it's too crowded!"). In either case, it shouldn't be about the numbers; it should be about whether the college matches up with you. If it doesn't, who cares if you get into a school that's not for you? But if it does …

… well, it's decision time. Truth is, many students don't get into these colleges because of luck — it 's because they saw what they wanted and went the many extra miles to get there. For example, a couple of these colleges ask if you've done any published research in high school. We're not talking a lab report or a winning science fair project; we're talking worked with a college professor on a new aspect of an old idea, and contributed enough that your name is in a respected scholarly journal somewhere.

At seventeen.

National champion debaters, the best cellist in the Eastern US, champion figure skaters, the winner of the World Math Decathlon — if their academic credentials are OK, where do you think they stand with other A students? That's not to say As aren't important, but when everyone who applies to a college has As, you can't blame the college for saying, as nicely but as clearly as possible, "Great. Do you have anything else?" And don't think you can escape by saying, "But I went to a great high school," since they'll tell you everyone else did, too — and they did.

If you think this can be devastating, you're right — that's why I'm mentioning it now. If you want to keep the option of a highly selective college open, you're wise to start pursuing your interests in ways others do not. This isn't about padding a college application with things that mean nothing to you; this is about enriching your life with something that means a great deal to you, and showing that care to the world at an amazing level. The hours of practice, the TV given up for summer programs, the time away from family — this is a demonstrated passion that's way more than giving up Saturday mornings for test prep. This is yet another version of living a rich, full life, about a level of commitment and achievement you just can't bluff.

It's certainly true that selective colleges take a lot of straight A students who weren't the ambassador to Spain at age 12, but if you look closely, you'll see way more students there who have sent the message that they know who they are, and who they are is seriously committed. No one will judge you if you shoot for this target and miss, or decide not to aim for it at all. The heads-up here is so you know what's expected if a highly selective college is calling to you, and so you won't judge yourself this way either.

Chapter 11

TALKING WITH YOUR PARENTS ABOUT COLLEGE

It's usually right about here that I catch it.

"Take my parents with me to visit colleges?
Dude, why don't you just tell me to take them to homecoming, too?"

I hear you — but here's the thing. As soon as you start taking tests and visiting colleges, most parents freak — they shouldn't (neither should you), but they do. It's like I said back in Chapter 1 — even though your parents will tell you college applications were a breeze for them, the minute it's about you, that cute pudgy baby in the widdle blanket, even the most laid back parent can start scoping the Internet for deals on test prep computer programs. In fairness, it's not always this way, but when it happens, it ain't fun, since now you have not only your college issues to deal with, you've got their's, too.

It's time to hold hands and cross the street together.

In addition to being a college counselor, I teach American Government, and one of the interesting things about government is that both sides can be right at the same time. It's the same thing with college; you want some space to sort things out, get (and keep) your head clear, and check out some schools. Cool. Your parents want you to have a good future, make sure you're safe, and be sure they aren't throwing college tuition away at some school where students go to more football games than classes. Fair enough.

The way you both get what you want is the weekly meeting. At the beginning of the college selection process, student and parents agree to meet once a week for twenty minutes to talk about college. During this twenty minutes, it's OK to ask about anything related to college. Your parents can ask if you're taking enough college prep classes, if any colleges are coming to visit your high school, if there is an application deadline coming up, if you made that appointment with your counselor — anything. At the same time, you can ask about anything, too —

why you have to apply to the college they went to, how they would feel if you took a year off before starting college, why they embarrassed you by asking that lame question at the last college tour — anything. Nobody loses their cool, nobody interrupts, and everybody ends the meeting knowing what they need to find out to answer someone else's questions; unless the answers are time sensitive, the answers are shared at the next meeting, which is the next time anyone gets to talk about college.

There's no hard and fast rule about when to start these meetings — some parents need to start them once the practice PLAN comes home, while others will stay calm until Labor Day of senior year — but if you want to score some major points, make sure you're the one who suggests the idea of starting weekly meetings. This will give your parents the correct impression that you've got your act together, and that you care about what they have to say. It will also give you a little more breathing room — once parents know you've got things under control, they're less inclined to clip your wings, and more inclined to let you fly.

I've seen a lot of students make great college plans on their own, but having the folks along to root you on is like T-ball — it's more fun to hit the ball knowing someone will cheer when you go yard. The weekly meeting will do that for you.

P.S. When you suggest the meetings, make sure your parents bring food.

Chapter 12
WORKING WITH YOUR COUNSELOR

In case you thought you were out of the woods, your parents aren't the only adults you have to help stay organized. Another one is your counselor.

Go ahead. I'll wait.

> *"Dog, not only do I have my own mess to keep straight, but now I have to put my parents and my counselor on my back? I don't even know who my counselor is, and they sure don't know me."*

Right — and that's the problem. If you look at most college applications, there's a part your counselor has to fill out, about the classes you've taken, your grades, and your class rank. There's also a spot where your counselor can make comments about you — the space may be small, but it's still there. One of three things will happen with this space: It stays blank; your counselor scribbles something in it that could describe anybody; your counselor has so many helpful things to say about you, they have to write "continued on attached sheet."

Two questions here. First, if you gave your counselor that form today, which option would they choose? Second, which one are you rooting for?

Sounds like you have work to do.

This isn't hard. For the first two years of high school, see your counselor when you need to — to change a schedule, discuss a personal problem, apply for a summer program — and, if they have time, talk about college. Like it or not, your counselor is way overworked — schedule changes, college counseling, career plans, and personal guidance for 500 students keeps them busy — so the great group counseling programs they run, and an occasional "hi" from you will go a long way in meeting both of your needs. So go if you need to; if not, space is cool.

The time to ramp things up is February of junior year. If your school is like most, your counselor will see you in March to put your senior schedule together. By the end of February (right — February), you want to type up your community service work and extra curricular activities from your notebook (remember your notebook?), along with awards and recognitions you've received. You also want to have your senior year schedule together before you have your scheduling meeting — read that again — and you want to put everything in an inexpensive pocket folder that has your name on it.

I hope you see where this is going. When it's time for your scheduling meeting, you hand over the folder, and start talking first.

> Hi, Mrs. Jones. I know you're really busy, so I got a copy of my transcript from your secretary and planned out my schedule already. I also wanted you to know I'm registered for the April SAT and ACT, and I'm visiting three colleges over spring break. I don't know if I'll see you before it's time to apply for colleges, so I've enclosed a list of my extra curriculars and community service projects, and I've highlighted the ones I'm most proud of. I've also put my cell phone number at the top of the page, so you can call me when you're filling out my applications if you have any questions. Thanks for helping me with this — if I have any questions, what's the best way to contact you?

I promise you — if you do this, your counselor will remember you, and look for excuses to see you from now on.

Counselor on track, counselor off back.

Nice work, dog.

Chapter 13
COLLEGE FAIRS

Having that conversation with your counselor at the end of 11th grade requires some serious prep time throughout the rest of 11th grade. There are four things you'll do junior year to make a good college choice, and the most important one is to visit more colleges. From Chapter 9, you know the basics of campus visits. As a junior, you'll need to look a little closer, a little longer, and a little harder ...

... but before you hit the campuses, you should do some homework at a local college fair. College visits cost time and money, and you'll need to make the most of both junior year. College fairs help you do that — held in fall and spring, a fair can have representatives from up to 400 colleges, all eager to talk to you about their college and your life. Many fairs feature information on choosing and applying to college and financial aid, and most fairs are free.

With so many colleges at a fair, it's easy to get intimidated — so plan ahead. Take a pen, a highlighter, an unofficial copy of your transcript, and five questions committed to memory that will help you learn more about a college. What you ask is up to you — majors, food, chances for research, cost, social life — just make sure the answers will help you decide if this place is worth a closer look.

At the fair, get a map of where the booths of the colleges are located. BEFORE you go onto the floor, highlight the colleges you're interested in. (This same list might be on a Web site — even better, since you can research colleges ahead of time.) Once you're at a booth, you might have to wait to ask questions — this is good! Use this time to listen to what the representative is saying to other students — since they will most likely be discussing general questions, you can use your time to ask more detailed stuff.

Once it's your turn, get busy. "Hi, my name is (NO student does this, but you should; it shows confidence, and gives the rep the chance to remember you), and I go to Captain Jack High School." From here, you want to ask your questions; make eye contact as they answer, and don't rush them.

If you feel you're hitting a good vibe, pull out your transcript and say "Just one more question. I'm putting my senior schedule together. Here's what I've taken so far; what other courses would your college like to see me take?" ABSOLUTELY, POSITIVELY NOBODY does this at a college fair, which is why you should. Most of the time, you'll actually get some great advice (or even a scholarship offer), but don't be surprised if they don't know what to say — either way, you'll be remembered by reps in a very positive way. Thank them for their time, fill out a registration card (that's important), tell them you hope they come by your school to visit, and move on.

Make quick notes on this college *before* you visit the next booth. You can use your "waiting time" at the next booth to do this, but write at least something down — you don't want to confuse your colleges.

If you can do about seven to 10 colleges and spend time at an information session of interest to you, call it a victory with an after-fair pizza (this is why you bring your parents along — to pay!) You now have some solid information on which colleges are road trip worthy, and some solid information about yourself as well — truly a dynamic duo.

Chapter 14
MORE SEARCH TOOLS

There are other great ways to scope out college possibilities without leaving home. Most of them are easy, all of them are helpful, and one popular one should be avoided — read on.

A great way to find out more about a college is to let the college come to you. Many colleges send admission representatives to your high school in the fall to tell you about their college. A list of these colleges is posted in the counseling center or the main office; every Thursday, write down the colleges that will be coming next week, look them up in your college guide (more on that soon), then get a pass from counseling to visit with the rep. In some high schools, reps are only allowed to come before or after school, or during lunch, and some will only let reps talk to students during lunch in the lunchroom (whoa — talk about leaving an impression!) If your school has these rules, give up the free time and go anyway — not many students will do this, which is (everybody sing along now) exactly why you should.

The same goes for hotel visits. Sometimes reps have such tight schedules they can only hold visits for lots of students at a hotel ballroom, in the evening or on weekends. The same rules apply here — do your homework, and go if it sounds good, bringing along your compadres and family for fun, along with dinner before or ice cream after. Whether it's in a hotel or the school's lunchroom, take along your college fair questions, fill out a card (even if you've talked to this rep or visited the campus before), introduce yourself to the rep (nothing like face time), ask a great question, and write down what you think once you're home.

If at any point you're not sure you're heading in the right direction, a college search might be helpful. *Collegeboard.com* lets you sort out colleges a million ways, from majors to location to activities to you name it. *Princetonreview.com* has the Counselor-O-Matic, which asks you questions to point you in the right direction. These sites and others can give you some general direction and lots of schools to consider.

Another great source is college guides — books or magazines that describe colleges and what they have to offer. Guides give you a solid look at all parts of a college; a good guide will tell you about classes, the campus, social life, and atmosphere, and a great guide will include interviews with students, who will give you the straight scoop. There are a lot of these around — try your counseling office or local public library ...

... but while you're there, avoid books or magazines with college rankings. College rankings are designed to tell you what the "best" colleges are, based on the opinion of someone who doesn't even know what you're looking for. Unfortunately, parents love this stuff, especially if the rankings include the opinions of university presidents.

Now, university presidents are nice people, but asking them to rank the 300 best colleges in the country is like asking your high school principal to rank the 300 best high schools in the country — after about 20 or so, they're relying more on what they've heard than what they know, and either way, they don't know you.

You don't need to read a magazine to find out Southwestern Michigan State is a great college; you need to find out if SMS is a great college for you. Guides will help you with that, and rankings won't — so save your time and money, and skip them.

Chapter 15

COLLEGE CONSIDERATIONS
FOR FINE AND PERFORMING ARTISTS

The most popular college guides, college fairs, and online search tools get many college seekers (not to be confused with Quidditch seekers) off to a good start, but these tools can leave some wannabe college wizards (not to be confused with – well, OK, you get the idea) looking for more. A History major is looking for a college that specializes in Renaissance History; an Anthropology major wants Forensic Anthropology ...

... and artists want something more than just a list of Art schools.

When it comes to help with niche (SAT word!) majors, naval architecture majors get pages of Web links on top schools; English horn majors get an article explaining why it's better to play English horn than oboe, but they get no clues on colleges that help them achieve this goal. Just ducky.

Serious high school artists are used to working a little harder to dig up the resources and opportunities they need to follow their passions, and college is no different. Dancers, painters, musicians and metal smiths alike would do well to connect these dots to find a college that will nurture the rhythm of their hearts:

Ask the right people. Most music, drama, dance and art teachers have to get a degree in their specialty, and the passionate teachers follow the current trends in college programs. Their insights into strong programs and your interests are a strong combination; the same is true if you take private lessons or study with someone outside of school. Polish this off with a trip to your counselor's office, and you're off to a good start; if they don't know, their connections to the arts community will get you an answer faster than you can say presto.

Go to the right college fairs. The National Association for College Admission Counseling (nacacnet.org) runs a series of Visual and Performing Arts fairs each fall. College reps at these fairs have special insights into the artistic offerings at their colleges, and can point you in the right direction.

Visual artists also have National Portfolio Days (*portfoliodays.net*), where you can take your work and get advice from art faculty and admissions officers on the work you've done to date and where to go from here. NPD events can be a little crowded, but they're worth the wait.

Look at general colleges, too. Artists often focus on institutes or conservatories that only offer degrees in music, art, etc., but it's wise to look closely at colleges or universities that have strong arts programs as part of a larger choice of majors. Not only are there some great arts programs at general colleges, they often provide substantial talent-based scholarships some institutes can't afford. A general U is also something to consider if you know you want art to be part of your life, but not your entire life or living. You don't have to decide right now, but it's wise to keep your options open; general colleges let you do that.

Review audition and portfolio requirements. Admission requirements for arts programs vary from a heavy reliance on academic classes to, "If you can draw, you're in." Since this mix varies widely from school to school — and since every school has different requirements for your audition or art portfolio — make sure you know what the expectations are for each school. Portfolios are usually submitted electronically as photographs of your work; ask your art teacher for the name of the top local art/tech person who has the magic touch in putting your work in its best light.

Chapter 16
COLLEGE CONSIDERATIONS FOR ATHLETES

Many students who want to play sports at college have been dreaming, thinking and preparing for their opportunity since well before high school. At the same time, there are too many stories about athletes losing eligibility or opportunities to play, even when it's not their fault.

To make sure you get on your field of dreams, start with these basics:

Know the rules. Most colleges belong to athletic associations with clear guidelines on eligibility, recruiting techniques, and students visiting colleges. The best known set of guidelines is for the NCAA, at ncaastudent.org; check with the colleges you're interested in to see the set of guidelines they have to follow, and make sure you (and your parents) read those guidelines at least once a month, starting from the time you contact a college (or are contacted) to the last day you play college ball.

Make sure you're academically eligible. Most colleges and athletic associations have minimum class, GPA, or test score requirements athletes have to meet in high school. Colleges may need transcripts and test scores to make sure you qualify; others will have you register with the NCAA Clearinghouse to confirm your ability to play. Make sure you do your part early, and keep your grades up to the very end, since eligibility GPAs are calculated to the very end of senior year.

Be clear on how to contact a college. Colleges don't always find quality athletes, so it's important to know when and how you should introduce yourself to a program. Most contacts include a letter or e-mail from you to the coach or athletic department. Since many colleges are cutting back on recruitment travel, it's wise to send a DVD of your work as an athlete, along with a resume of your teams, championships, and awards. Camera stores and professional videographers can put these "highlight reels" together for a fee that's well worth it — your coach can point you in the right direction.

Going to campus? Plan ahead. Visiting a potential college is a must for all students, especially athletes, but colleges will sometimes offer to pay an athlete's way to campus. There are limits on when and how often a college can do this, along with when and how often they can be in contact. Make sure you don't fumble a choice away by not knowing what you — or they — should and shouldn't do.

Get a clear understanding of their commitment. One student thought she was getting a guaranteed volleyball scholarship, when in fact she was one of 14 freshmen trying to get three slots on the varsity. She didn't make it, so her scholarship ended after one year. Since her family couldn't afford the tuition, she came home.

Getting an offer to join a team — or better yet, a scholarship to join the team — is a real head rush and cause for celebration. After the initial thrill wears off, read the offer as closely as you would a financial aid offer (see Chapter 47); if you don't know what the offer really means, ask the college. If you're still unclear, ask a counselor, your coach, or an attorney.

Get a clear understanding of your commitment. College athletes often have to meet with tutors and attend required study halls, in addition to going to class and practices that can take five or six hours out of every day. This level of discipline is often more than what a student wants to give; once you know the college is willing to stand by their end of the agreement, make sure you're ready to stand by yours.

Chapter 17
COLLEGE CONSIDERATIONS FOR STUDENTS WITH SPECIAL NEEDS

A successful college search for a student — any student — leads them to colleges that will offer the right mix of challenge and support. Also known as "fit," this is why water polo players who want to major in Chinese only apply to certain colleges; same for students who may need extra time on tests, an interpreter that knows sign language, or a dorm room they can share with their leader dog.

Everyone is entitled to the college fit that's best for them. To make sure you're customizing your college search to include as many choices as possible, follow these important steps:

Talk to you counselor early. All students should spend time talking college with their counselor, but if you have a special need, ask for help early and often. The answers you need may be best found by having your counselor ask other counselors; give them the time and the chance to help.

Ask the teachers in your resource center. The aides and teachers helping you in high school have probably worked with other students with similar needs who went to college. Use their wisdom to help guide you in the right direction; they may even be able to connect you with former students who can give you the inside story on what to look for in a college.

Request SAT and ACT accommodations. More and more students are having their learning needs met on college tests; both offer services that include extra time, extra breaks, readers, and large-type test booklets. You'll need to apply early, and most requests will require some kind of documentation. Talk to your counselor to see who can help you complete the paperwork, and when (and how often) it needs to be filed.

Head for the Web. Do an online search for "Colleges for Students With (ADHD, Dyslexia, Asperger's)", and you will find a treasure trove of options. Like all Web searches, you need to be choosy; the best lists tend to come from associations that offer a wide array of services for students (Asperger Foundation International, etc.) or well-established college search sites. Keep looking at lists until you start to see the same colleges mentioned three or four times; that's the beginning of a strong list.

Hit the books. A tour through your local (or online) bookstore will show a number of guides and books that will identify possible colleges, and offer advice on how to reach your goal of going to college. A popular place to begin is *The K&W Guide to Colleges for Students with Learning Disabilities*. This guide tends to focus on larger public institutions, but combined with information on college Web sites, it can help you frame the questions you need to ask every college, big and small.

Visit, visit, visit. Like every college search, books, Web sites, and the advice of others only go so far. This is especially true of college searches for special needs students; while colleges list what they offer, students usually find a great variation in the accommodations offered by different teachers at different colleges — even the colleges considered to be leaders in supporting special needs students. Your campus visit must include time to talk with students whose needs are like yours; just like fellow Biology majors, the students know what the college really has to offer.

In addition, know that you'll have to speak up for yourself at any college campus. The art and science of asking for what you need is a life skill you should hone now. It's the best way to make sure you'll start, finish, and enjoy college.

Chapter 18

ACT AND SAT

As you're scoping out college visits, you'll have to set aside a couple of Saturday mornings for college testing. I know you'd rather spend Saturday morning in fuzzy pajama bottoms and a T-shirt your parents won't let you wear to school, but sometimes we make sacrifices in the name of higher education, and this is one of those times.

The testing ground rules should be familiar. You know what the SAT looks like from your PSAT testing; ditto for the ACT and your PLAN testing. One big difference is that the SAT and ACT contain writing sections, where you have to write an actual essay on a topic they give you, at the test site, in about 25 minutes. The writing test is optional on ACT, but take it — you don't want to find the school of your dreams this summer, only to discover they require the ACT writing test you didn't take this spring.

If you're trying to figure out which test to take, that's easy — take both in February or April of junior year. It's likely you'll score much better on one test than the other, but your PSAT and PLAN scores don't really predict which test that will be. Once you know which one you can groove on, you might want to take it again in June of your junior year, just to make sure you've done your best. You don't have to worry which test is required by the colleges of your dreams; every college that recruits nationally will take either the ACT or the SAT — so figure out the one that's best for you, and work from your strength.

Registration for both tests is best done online, at *www.collegeboard.org* (SAT) and *www.act.org* (ACT). Sample test questions are online too; if you need more, bookstores sell additional samples. The real tests aren't cheap, but they cost a whole lot more if you miss a deadline and register late — so pay attention now, or pay serious cash later (a limited number of fee waivers are also available for these tests — see your counseling office.) Since April is a big test date, register for April early in your junior year. Not every high school gives the tests, and if all the test sites close to you are full, you may have to drive a while (like, to a different state!) to take them. If you want to qualify for extra time or accommodations, start very early.

In addition to ACT and SAT, there is yet another breed of test — the SAT Subject Tests. Unlike the SAT (aka, the SAT Reasoning Test), these tests are only an hour long, and measure your understanding of a specific subject — things like Biology, Math, and Foreign Language. Some colleges want you to take two or three of these tests, in addition to taking the ACT or the Reasoning SAT. Most of these colleges will let you decide which Subject Tests to take, but some will require specific ones (like Math if you're an Engineering Major). Since the requirements vary from school to school and year to year, check the college's Web site to get their requirements — then check again in August before senior year to make sure they haven't changed.

You sign up for these tests at the same Web site as SAT, and since the tests are only one hour long, you can take up to three tests on the same Saturday morning — leaving more time for jammieology, which, regrettably, is not a college major — at least not an official one, anyway.

Chapter 19
TEST PREP

Registering for the tests is easy — the harder part is getting ready for them. There are a zillion options here, including a couple I bet you haven't thought of. Here we go:

- **Timing.** SAT and ACT are designed to measure what students know in the spring of the junior year. Some students take these tests earlier than spring, but I'd be careful — you might not know all of the math or English on the tests if you take them sooner. Also, remember that you can take the tests in fall of your senior year if necessary, through December.

  With SAT Subject Tests, the timing may be different. Most students take these as seniors, in October or December — it spreads the testing out — but if you're not taking a Biology class when you're taking the Biology test, you may be rusty. Using a test prep booklet solves this, so long as you have the discipline to use it — if not, take the test at the end of the class.

- **Re-testing.** Some people get ready for a test by taking it over and over ... and over! Scores do tend to go up in the second testing, but not much after that, unless you study. So seven times is out, unless you need a specific score to nail a scholarship.

- **Self-help.** Between the sample tests, test prep booklets, Web sites, and computer programs, there are all kinds of ways to study at your own pace — but will you? It's easy enough to say you'll study on Saturday or after homework's done; most students need a parental assist with this. ("You can have your cell phone back once you've studied for an hour!")

- **Classes.** Some classes teach you the content of the test; others show you strategies; others do both. Some run two days; others run 14 weeks. Some are outrageously expensive; others are less outrageously expensive. If you go this route, ask for specific data — "You say your average student raises their test scores 400 points. What's the average for students who had PSAT scores like mine?" Also, ask about class scholarships, or discounts for students from the same high school.

- **Tutors.** Take your PSAT or PLAN results to an experienced tutor, and in a few sessions, they can work with you on the areas you most need help in. You don't waste time with a class that overviews the whole test, and it can be cheaper than a full blown class to boot. This works even better if you bring April ACT or SAT results in to prep for the next exams.

- **Apply to a "No Test" College.** If you think testing doesn't really tell a college anything about you, you're not alone. Over 800 colleges don't use SAT or ACT as part of the admissions process for most of their students; these include some highly selective schools, and the list gets larger every year. If this testing strategy sounds right for you, buzz by *http://www.fairtest.org/optstate.html* to look at the list of schools, then double-check on the Web site of the college you're interested in.

The College Freak Factor is mighty high when it comes to test prep — most students either freak about the tests and do way too much studying, or they freak about having to give up free time and do way too little. You have to do what's comfortable, and what you can afford in money and time, but this is the one area where many former students say, "If I had to do anything different, I would have studied more."

Just notice they said study — not obsess.

Chapter 20

SENIOR SCHEDULE AND MORE ON COLLEGE VISITS

By March, you're registered for (or taken) the ACT and SAT, and you have at least three colleges you'd like to visit. That leaves two things left to do — senior schedule, (see below), and asking teachers to write you letters of recommendation (see Chapter 30).

Your senior schedule has to do three things:

1. *Have all the classes you need to graduate.* One key to getting into college is to get out of high school, so double check your transcript, make sure you are literally good to go, and count your gym credits twice — they're slippery.

2. *Keep you challenged all of senior year.* Speaking of gym, remember what coach said — play to the whistle. If you take a soft schedule, you'll forget about thinking, studying, writing, and organizing your time. You'll then spend the first semester of college remembering these things, along with learning how to do laundry, getting yourself out of bed, and calling your parents often enough that they'll remember you at Thanksgiving. A bad start in college is like a bad start in 9th grade — it's tough to catch up. You're in shape, so stay in shape — just say no to schedule sludge. If you've run out of tough classes in high school, take some at a local college — in some states, your high school will even pay for the courses.

3. *Show the colleges you're serious about learning.* The trained pigeons schedule hard classes for three years of high school, and maybe the first half of senior year, but then — out comes six sections of The History of Pizza. The college of your dreams will see this epidemic of senioritis on your final transcript — yes, you have to send them one — and if your grades go down a lot (say, A- average to B-), or if your schedule is soft, they'll think you've changed your mind about learning, so they might change their mind about you. Try it if you dare — it happens.

With the goals of junior year behind us, let's revisit visiting colleges. Some students have big dreams about faraway colleges — you wouldn't believe how many juniors in Michigan ask about University of Hawaii — but they can't get there to visit. In addition, many families can't afford to visit colleges, even if they aren't across the ocean. They can visit the local schools on their list, but the distant ones are a stretch.

Fair enough — it's time for Plans B and C of college visits. Plan B is simple — wait until April of senior year to visit colleges. By then, you'll know which ones you've been admitted to, so the number you'll visit will be smaller. Since this eliminates your ability to see potential colleges as a junior, this plan isn't perfect, but there might be enough local colleges to give you a good taste of the different kinds of colleges that are out there.

Plan C is even simpler — let someone else help pay for it. If one of your pals is heading out for a campus tour by car, offer to pay for gas and go with them. If you're worried their opinion might bias you, talk about that before you go — a true friend will understand, and you'll be able to work something out.

If you're the first in your family to go to college, or a member of an underrepresented ethnic group, the college might actually pay for your visit. Fly-in programs are becoming a big deal to even small colleges, and all you have to do is ask and fill out a form. Now that's a bargain.

Chapter 21
MAKING THE LIST

Dudes and dudettes, it's time to chill. Put on your favorite workout shorts, grab a box of cereal, borrow one of your mom's scented candles (no dude — not the one that plugs into the wall), put on your John Coltrane CD, and crash on the couch.

At this stage of things, you're heading into the home stretch. By studying hard, giving back, thinking about your place in the world, and having fun, your high school years have been da bomb and da bedrock — something to build on, not just for a college application, but for applying yourself once you're in college, and once you're out. Because you built up over time, you're not burned out over college; because your parents and your counselor are in the queue (SAT word!), they're not on your case; because you've visited colleges, you're focused on finding one that's right for you, instead of finding one that's "right."

You'll need to hold on to that last thought really tight from now until next June. Lots of well-meaning folks at the family reunion, the church barbecue, or the Custard Cone will ask you where you're going to go, and what you're going to major in. If you don't give them the answer they want to hear — that you'll be majoring in business at a name college — they will do things with their face you could have sworn were limited to cartoon characters who eat too many Cocoa Doodles for breakfast. (Go easy on those, OK?)

Of course, it's fine to major in business at a name college — if that's what's right for you — but if that's not where you are, then that's not where you should go. Don't get me wrong — the last thing you want to do is head to college without thinking about your plans. But if you've thought about your plans and you don't have a major, then finding a college that will let you look around a while is a plan, even if it's at a college no one's heard of, and even if you change your major a lot once you're there (which most students do — even the business majors.)

Keeping your focus amid all of those opinions, mosquitoes, and charred burgers might not be easy — so you need to focus on something else. As you start your transition summer, as you continue to visit colleges, remember your goal is to come to the first day of senior year with two things:

1. A killer tan (cool — but use sun screen!)

2. A list of four to eight colleges you'd like to apply to, which includes:

    a. at least one college in your home state;

    b. two colleges with average grades and test scores that are equal to yours, or even a little lower;

    c. a couple of dream schools you can't quite figure out how you'll get into or pay for;

    d. all colleges you'd be happy to go to.

We'll talk more about the list over the next few chapters, as I offer you some ideas about college options you probably haven't considered. For now, dream on, be strong in the work you have done so far ...

... and blow out that candle, ace. That pine smell is doing me in!

Take some time right now down your current list, and look at it every day this summer.

Chapter 22
SAFETY SCHOOLS AND TRANSFERRING

Most students don't beef about applying to an in-state school. If you've visited local campuses, you've probably found a college that will work for you if you stay close to home, either to be near family, or because instate public schools are a bargain. You might have the heart of a Rainbow Warrior (remember that University of Hawaii thing?), but hearts are funny things, and by April being a Sooner or a Spartan or a Hustlin' Quaker may be just as wonderful, even though home is just an hour away — or because home is just an hour away.

The real hustle I get (with Quakers or not) is when I tell students to apply to two safety schools — places where, based on test scores and GPA, you're in the middle of the pack, if not a little ahead. Students find nice ways to express their concern about this, but it basically boils down to this:

Holmes, why would I want to go to a school
where I'm the smartest student?

I get that. Good students want challenge, and they think the best way to get challenge is from students who are smarter than they are. Other students think a degree from a college nobody's heard of won't help much when it comes to landing jobs or getting into med school.

So why safety schools? First, knowing you've found a college you like and can get into (and a safety school has to be both) gives you confidence — it's the rock you build on while completing applications to more selective colleges. September might tell you it's cool just to apply to tough schools, but February and March seem colder than usual if every application that might be a yes could just as easily (or more likely) be a no. Safety schools school you on how applications work, and give you the "Yes!" factor you need to take on applications with 86 parts.

Second, dough and prestige (no ma'am, that's one reason, not two — but thanks for asking!). Lots of competitive colleges offer automatic scholarships to students with high grades or test scores. Right — you get bucks no matter who you are, whether you need them or not. In addition, a student who's stronger than most can find their way into a good college's honors program or advanced scholars courses. This means smaller classes, better profs, and fellow students who can rip it up in the classroom. You're looking for someone to set the pace, and programs with grad school horsepower? Gentle dudes, start your engines!

Finally, there's the two college strategy. Highly selective colleges are crazy competitive — the main reason students get rejected is because the college runs out of room. Since very small differences make the difference, some students make a different plan — start at a safety school, and transfer to the dream school.

You have to be careful here — most highly competitive colleges are even harder to get into as a transfer, and you have to watch the classes you take at School #1, since not all will transfer. This also means you have to go through the application process twice, and deadlines for transfers are different. Still, this is a growing trend — stay local, stoke the GPA, save some dough, and off you go. Also, if you transfer enough college credits, they might not look at your high school grades at all — and sometimes a new start is very cool. Transfer is also an option if your dream school turns out to be a nightmare. Either way, watch your classes, stay organized, get great grades …

… and hustle on, Quakers!

Chapter 23
IS COLLEGE WORTH IT?

It's May of your junior year, and you have so much to do, you think your head will explode. Papers to write, ACTs to take, letters of recommendation to ask for, and your summer job plans have just fallen through. You open your e-mail, and you've received your schedule for next year: Five academic classes, one honors class, and two APs. If all goes well, you'll be admitted to a college that's right for you, where you'll get to do this for four more years.

"Dude," you say to yourself, "is college worth it?"

Your parents come back from a dinner party in the neighborhood. "I ran into Jenny Smithers" your Mom says. "She graduated from State U this spring with Honors in Architecture, but with the slow housing market, she's working as an assistant manager at Burger World and living at home."

"She's the eighth college grad in the neighborhood who came back home," says Dad. "One more, and the unemployed college grads can start a baseball team."

"Dude," you say to yourself, "is college worth it?"

You take a break from studying to catch the end of the golf match on TV. As you're flipping the channels, you stop at a story that talks about Bill Gates, Abe Lincoln, and some woman in Connecticut. The story says Bill Gates didn't finish college and Abe Lincoln never started, but this woman in Connecticut took out $115,000 in loans to go to college. She now has a Bachelor's Degree in Philosophy, and can't get a job.

"Dude," you say to yourself.

You head back to the computer, and make a scientific investigation. It turns out that the unemployment rate is lowest for students with college degrees. It also turns out that most of the job growth in the next 10 years will come in jobs requiring training after high school, but not a four year degree. It also turns out the average graduate with a Bachelor's Degree has $30,000 in college loans.

"Whoa!" says you.

You've decided your homework can wait, and you head down to Maggie's Pizza. Dave's the manager on duty tonight, and he's the smartest guy you know.

"'Sup, bro?" he says, without looking up from the pizza he's cutting.

"Dave, is college worth it?" Dave looks up, puts down the pizza cutter, and wipes his hands on his apron.

"Let's see. Moved in the day before classes started, and I was so scared, I didn't unpack til November 12. My roommate was from Brooklyn, and he taught me how to eat pizza the right way. Read my first book of poetry. Worked my summers cleaning dorm rooms, and swore I'd never do that again. Went to Scotland for three weeks, and got to see the sun set at midnight. Learned how to footnote a paper, why camels spit, how to write the business plan that led to this store and the four others in the chain, and why it matters to me who wins the elections in Turkey."

"What happened November 12th?"

"I met Maggie."

"Hmm."

"What about you, man? You know what you want to study?"

"No."

"Where you want to live?"

"No."

"Do for a living?"

"No."

"Yeah. That's about where I was, before I went. Slice to go?"

Dave shows you how to eat pizza Brooklyn style, and you head for home.

"Where've you been, champ? There's homework to do."

"Sorry, Dad. Just needed to clear my head."

"Well, it's a busy time for you."

"Yeah. Hey, Dad?"

"Yes?"

"Who's running for president in Turkey?"

Chapter 24

HAVE YOU CLEANED UP YOUR FACEBOOK PAGE YET?

There are three key technology rules when it comes to applying to college:

1. If at all possible, use the college's online application, and ask their tech support for help the minute you run into a problem.

2. Create a new e-mail account just for the messages that will be sent to and from colleges.

3. Clean up any and all social media pages you have .

Students understand the first two with no problem. College applications need to be clear, clean and thorough, so it's important to make sure you're uploading your college essays, not your prom pictures.

Ditto for a new e-mail account. E-mail may be old school to you, but this is how most colleges contact you, even once you enroll. This makes it easy to keep track of college contacts, and it's probably all for the best colleges not know your personal e-mail address is *ladiesgoforme@mymail.com.*

But try and talk the plusses of Web site maintenance, and students are convinced you roamed the Earth with dinosaurs. They insist colleges don't care about social media accounts, and are too busy to check them — to prove it, they'll actually ask colleges if they look, and the colleges will say no.

Fair enough — except when I asked a college if they looked, their answer was, "Do you really think I'd tell you if we did?"

Play it safe. Rough language, risky pictures — even having an account under another name — can hurt you and anyone else who's in those questionable photos with you. Once you've tidied up yours, ask your friends to take anything about you that's iffy off their pages, too. After that, search for yourself on the Web, and see what's there. You might not need to address it or be able to do anything about it, but it's better for you to know before the colleges do.

And even if the colleges don't look, they sometimes find out in very strange ways that can do serious damage…

(Based on a true story that happened somewhere else.)

Joanna thought she was all that
She knew she was a winner;
A 3.9, a 32
The gal was no beginner!
Took five APs and tutored, too
Her homework was a snap
Spent most nights on the Facebook page
Just dishin' out some smack
She posted pix of homecoming
Her folks would see as knockouts
But dog, they'd never seen them, since
Her FB page was blocked out.

You can't imagine her surprise
When her counselor said, "Yo lady,
I got a call from East Coast U
The news will make ya crazy!
The U was ready to admit
When in arrived their intern
'The buzz is all on Facebook, man,
These pics will make your hands burn.'
The intern loaded up the page
Of some homecoming hijinx
And in the photo, there was you —
Which made our rep do eye blinks.

"They saw your pictures once or twice
And thought they'd overlook it
But then they read your FB smack
And that's what really cooked it.
Your essays were all erudite
And very nicely tailored
But then they saw the real you
Has language like a sailor.
They read your app and loved you girl,
It's you they were admittin',
But now they said they just can't take
A profane party kitten."

So dudes and dudettes, hear me out,
Few colleges go lookin',
But if FB vibes come their way
That just can't be mistooken
Your full ride dough, your dream admit
Are goin' down the tank, sir
And all because you tried to be
A bad-selfed Facebook gangsta!

Chapter 25

COMMUNITY COLLEGES AND GRADE POINT AVERAGES

Another player in the two college game is community colleges.

OK, OK. Are you through now?

"Junior college? Isn't that where they teach, like,
dog grooming and motorcycle safety?"

First of all, they aren't called junior colleges anymore — if you're looking for someone to say that name was a bad idea, my hand is raised. Second, yes, some CCs do teach dog grooming and cake decorating (hopefully not in the same classroom at the same time) ...

... and you should be very glad they do. Community colleges were based on this wacky notion that learning shouldn't be over at 22. Time goes by, and people change; the job you loved at twenty-five is boring at 34, or doesn't pay enough, or is gone. More school.

You thought school was dull, so you got a job after high school and made a ton of money. But now the magic of money has faded (it does that, youngsters), and you've found something you really want to do. More school.

You're at a four-year college, but you can't get all of your required classes. Summer vacation is coming up, but you want to get back on track to finish your degree on time. More school.

Lots of people in your community have a need for more school. The needs aren't the same, but the need for a local college is the same — that's why everyone voted for special taxes to build a college that's down the street and dirt cheap, with classes that give people new hobbies, new careers, new outlooks on life, and transferable credits to four year colleges (who often give CC transfer students with good grades great scholarships). From working on your GPA to working to make a dream come true, community colleges can be your best friend for now and for life — and learning for life is what this book is all about.

So no more woofin' about community colleges — dog!

And now, it's time to learn about GPA.

Your high school may have a grading system that requires the average person to use two calculators and a blender to figure out a GPA. As in, Honors classes add .3, Bs in AP courses add .28, Bs in Honors AP courses add .32, Cs in Accelerated Honors AP courses taught in the Winter semester lose .46 …

Many colleges want to compare all students using the same grading system, so they have to take out the different things high schools do to grades and treat them all the same. This is great, except that one college's version of "same" is different from another college's version of "same" — just like high school grading scales are different from one another.

Confused? Join the club.

As they think about senior schedule, students ask if getting Bs in AP classes is better than As in regular classes. If you look at the college options as a group, the answer is "it depends." If you look at my answer in Chapter 2, the answer is to take the most challenging classes you can. Unless you have one "dream school" that has a special GPA formula, I'd stick with Chapter 2.

Also — if a college says it's looking for a GPA of 3.5, that's based on whatever formula the college uses. This is one reason why students with 3.3s shouldn't hesitate to apply to a 3.5 college — you never know what your recalculated GPA will look like, unless you understand the way all of your colleges will treat your grades.

(Of course, if you do know, skip college and go work for NASA — you're rocket scientist material!)

Chapter 26

APPLICATION DEADLINES

In addition to thinking about in-state schools, safety schools, transfer schools, and GPAs, you might want to think about applying to a college based on when you'll hear back from them. This menu has five different entrees:

First come, first served (Rolling admissions). The sooner your application is complete at a rolling admissions college, the sooner they will read it and make a decision. If you'd like some security, you might want to consider applying to a safety school that's rolling; in some cases, you can hear by October if you apply in September.

First come, first served, sort of (Early Action, or EA). EA gives you an early date — usually November 1st — to turn in a completed application. All applications received by that date are read together, and decisions go out early. With EA, you hear earlier, but you still have until May 1st to decide if you want to go there.

First committed, first served (Early Decision, or ED). ED is like EA, but with a REALLY important addition. Like EA, you apply early, and you hear early. However, if you apply ED and are accepted, you MUST ATTEND THAT COLLEGE. Once an ED school says yes, you withdraw your applications to all other colleges. The only exception (and this is only sometimes) is if the college can't meet all of your financial need. If they can, you've found your new home.

First come and first committed, first served (Early Action Single Choice) Early Single Choice is just like EA, except a college that offers Early Single Choice limits the number of early applications you can make to one — just them. If the college takes you, you still have until May 1st to decide to go there — but you are limiting your early choices by applying to that school.

Y'all come, y'all served (Regular Admissions). These programs establish a common deadline (usually January 1st) and all applications are read at the same time. Decisions usually come out around April 1st.

Since some colleges have both an early program and a regular program, you might have to figure out which way to apply. Early programs give you the advantage of showing a college you're really interested in them, especially an ED application — but of course, if ED takes you, you have to go, and that commitment might be too big for you.

Many colleges take a large number of students from early programs, where the number of applications is small — so applying early may be to your advantage. Some early applicants may be deferred, where the college decides to review you with the later applicants. You may get in later, but you may not — if you're deferred, treat it like a waitlist (see the last three paragraphs of Chapter 51).

If you think the math of early programs is as complicated as the math of recalculating GPAs, you're on the right track. Advice on applying early varies greatly from college to college, but the general rule of thumb is you should apply early if a school is a top choice for you — in the case of an ED application, THE choice. Since many colleges with early programs are dropping them, this may be less of a big deal soon; either way, I'd find at least one safety school that does rolling admission, get that admission letter in my back pocket, and then take on the math of early versus regular.

No matter the program, remember that deadlines are stone cold real. An application that's due January 1st won't get read if it arrives January 2nd — so plan ahead.

Chapter 27

COLLEGE COSTS

Now that you're working on your final list, you (or your parents) are probably thinking about paying for college. This is bad, bad, good and bad:

It's bad if you decide not to scope out a school or apply just because you think it costs too much. You visit colleges to find out as much about you and what you like as you do to find out about the college. A trip to Megabucks College could lead to the discovery that you love archaeology, and that can lead you to dig up (get it — archaeology? Dig up?) other great archaeology schools that cost less. If you don't make the trip, you don't discover a part of yourself — talk about a high price!

It's also bad to pass on the high end, because the high end might be cheaper. A parent called to scold me for encouraging her senior to apply to a college they couldn't afford, and urged me to "encourage" their daughter to go to a local public college instead. The pricey school was perfect for the student, and she applied, hoping to get one of the college's full scholarships. There were only 10 available, but that didn't matter, because she only needed the one she got — and suddenly, school was free.

At the same time, it's good to build your list of colleges with money in mind. The student did indeed apply to that affordable public college, and would have been happy there — a perfect safety school. A few big cost colleges on your list is fine; all big cost colleges means you might be looking more at name and prestige than the things that really matter, like major, fit, and reality. Dream? You bet — but a dream is just one kind of vision, and putting together a good list requires insights of many kinds.

Finally, it's bad if now is the first time your parents are considering how to pay for college. Like most big expenses, planning ahead is good, even though doing that is often more jarring than putting it off and hoping things will work out — because sometimes, they don't. If your parents have a financial planner — no, that wouldn't be Al the lottery ticket guy at Speedy Mart — it's long past time for a visit. They should set up a meeting, without you, right away; in fact, that's a good idea for parents who have planned ahead, too. Mention it at your next weekly meeting ...

... and take along *www.finaid.org* with you. There's a lot to know — that you have to file with the Federal government to get anything from just about anyone, that you can't file with the Feds until after January 1st of senior year, that your college has other forms to fill out, that too much loan is bad. Finaid.org will get you through it all, in simple language, along with the biggest scholarship database in the history of the planet. You fill out a survey, give them your e-mail, and voila — you get a list of (usually) 200 scholarships you can apply for. When new scholarships come in, or scholarship deadlines are coming up, they e-mail you to let you know. They also have some great articles about scholarships scams, and why you should never have to pay to be eligible for a scholarship, or to find out about them.

It's true that money is a tool with power — but so is a chainsaw, and that isn't getting in your way of finding a great school. Like all power tools, treat it with respect, and you'll be fine.

Chapter 28

THE 20-MINUTE MEETING ON PAYING FOR COLLEGE

Most students read the last chapter and say,

> *"OK, so I have to find a couple of colleges I can afford*
> *and want to go to. Cool."*

Most parents read the last chapter and swear it's only 100 words long — like chocolate-covered potato chips, they just can't get enough information when it comes to paying for college.

Since they've paid for all of your schooling (and everything else) so far, and will most likely continue to do so, the least you can do is talk them through this. Here's the script for your next 20-minute meeting:

First, go directly to *http://www.finaid.org/calculators/finaidestimate.phtml*. This provides an estimate of what you would probably have to pay for college next fall. Note that I used the words "estimate" and "probably" in the same sentence — so this isn't a sure thing, but it's as close as it gets for now.

Second, check out your EFC, or Expected Family Contribution. This is approximately the amount of money you'll pay at most colleges, no matter what their tuition is (did you get "approximately" and "most"?) If your EFC is $15,000, and State U costs $20,000, you'll pay $15,000, and State U will try to put together a financial aid package to cover the rest. If East Coast U costs $45,000, chances are you'll still only pay around $15,000, and they will find more aid to cover the balance. Right — both colleges will most likely cost you about the same amount of money, although you'll need more travel money to get home from East Coast College.

Be careful. If you think this may make expensive colleges more affordable to you, you're right — it may. Since East Coast College has to find more money for you, there's a great chance their offer will include more loan, and more money you have to work off by getting an on-campus job (aka "work study"). Just how much loan and work study you get depends on each college — and you'll have to pay or work off those parts of the package. When you visit a college, ask these questions:

What is the complete cost (room and board, books, travel) of attendance, and what is your average financial aid package? Don't be surprised if private colleges tell you their package is around $25,000 — it's not uncommon.

What is the average debt a student graduates with — in other words, how much loan do most students roll up at that college?

Do they meet full financial need — in other words, if you need $30,000, will they find $30,000, or will there be a "gap" you have to come up with?

Next, take a peek at *www.meritaid.org*. Many students look for colleges that offer aid based on grades or test scores. *Meritaid.org* shows you many of these colleges, but if you find a dream college that offers merit aid, be sure to double check with the college — and remember, these scholarships are very competitive.

Many colleges are changing financial aid policies, including eliminating loans — and others may do so soon. Most college Web sites also offer financial aid calculators, but these are relatively new, so there may be a few kinks in them; run your numbers through them and through the finaid.org calculator, and if you end up with different answers, ask the college why.

Finally, remember you have to apply for financial aid every year. Your income changes and the price of college changes, so new numbers are always needed; add this to your list of New Year's resolutions for the next four years.

Chapter 29

THE 20 MINUTE MEETING AFTER THAT
(COLLEGE COSTS, PART 3)

Now that you've found a way to talk to your parents about college costs, there's a good chance they will want to talk to you about college costs — and if you think they were sweating a lot when you had the "birds and bees" discussion, just wait.

It's hard for parents to talk to their children about money for college — heck, it's hard for adults to talk to anyone about money. College is a particularly tough issue because most families don't save as much for college as they should, so when it comes time to pay for college, they're a little short — sometimes more than a little short. Since parents can see college is coming up sooner or later (it's not like the dishwasher breaking down out of the blue), this can lead to some serious parental guilt: I'm an awful parent; I don't make enough money; my life has been a failure.

Help your parents by focusing on the subject at hand. "OK, so the financial aid calculator says we can afford this much. With the savings we both have and the money we can make at work, is this realistic?" Note that the conversation here is about "we"; if your parents want to talk about paying for college, that's the first sign they can't do it alone. This may be a surprise, and it would have been better if they had told you this earlier, but you are where you are, and the only way to move forward is together. Stay focused for now; you can kick the garden gnome later.

On top of this, remember paying for college is about what you know and what you don't know. Colleges will offer financial aid packages with different amounts of grant and loan — packages you haven't seen yet. You may or may not go on to graduate school, so the amount of loan will have to be small — unless you're going into a field where your salary will be large enough that you can afford to pay back those loans

— but you aren't sure what your major will be. Your parents will want to retire someday, and not have to eat mac and cheese for every meal. What's that going to cost?

A key to dealing with the unknown is time. Your parents may need a breather after this meeting, which will give them a chance to get some help (suggest they call a financial planner) and some answers — give it to them.

Scour *www.finaid.org* and your counseling office for scholarships, and apply for all of them (more on that later).

Once you're admitted, compare financial aid packages closely, and if you have questions, or if you think the college doesn't understand your whole financial picture, CALL THEM — these folks are human, very humane, and will do everything ethically possible to find you college cash.

Once you're in college, look for cash that isn't advertised. Students can become lab assistants or dorm advisers after freshmen year, and these jobs often pay well, up to full room and board. Other off campus jobs may pop up based on what you learn and who you talk to freshman year. Keep looking, keep listening …

… and don't give up on a college right now just because it seems out of reach. It takes more than one person to make most dreams come true, and Mom and Dad are already on board. Build your list with two affordable colleges as the base, and let the other colleges help you as much as they can. You're doing your part; let them do theirs.

Chapter 30

LETTERS OF RECOMMENDATION — THE BIG PICTURE

Now that your list is complete, it's time to get busy. Not every college requires letters of recommendation — in fact, there are more that don't want letters than those that do. At the same time, having at least one letter of recommendation (I recommend two) is a good idea:

- It may help you get admitted. Colleges that don't ask for letters usually don't mind if you send one. If you're applying to a college where your grades and test scores make you a "maybe", extra words of support from a teacher who knows you well are right there for the admissions committee to consider — and those can push you over the top.

- You may change your mind soon. Suppose you stop by a college on your way home from Aunt Marge's over Thanksgiving weekend, and you love the place — but it requires letters of recommendation and has a December 1st deadline. If you plan ahead for the possible, your letters are waiting for you, and your dream stays alive.

- You may change your mind later on. If you transfer colleges or put college off for a while, your college may still want recommendations from high school. If you ask the teachers to write those letters now, they'll write about you based on fresh memories, not based on how they remember you two years from now — and for as much as they like you, time can make a difference.

- You may need it for money. Once you're through applying for colleges, you'll probably be filling out scholarship applications. Many scholarship applications require letters of recommendation, and having one that's ready to go can make all the difference in finding cash for college.

Some students freak about asking for letters — it's easy. In the spring of junior year, you've asked your teachers privately if they would write you a good letter of recommendation. The word "good" is important — any teacher can write you a letter, but if it's just going to be a list of your accomplishments and grades, that won't help. You want a letter from someone who knows you as a person and as a student — that makes a good letter. If the teacher honestly feels they can't write you a good letter, they'll tell you that in a gentle way. Don't be crushed — they're really helping you, since weak letters of recommendation are usually worse than no letters at all ...

... and this goes back to looking at the big picture. Just like applying to college isn't just about college, asking teachers for letters of recommendation isn't just about filling out forms. If you've really been making the most of high school, if you've been living and learning instead of only getting good grades, you're sure to have at least two or three teachers who didn't simply grade your papers and check your attendance. You'll also have learned about life from mentors, the teachers you formed relationships with, the ones who kept an eye out for you, who taught you right from wrong, or something else about the way the world worked.

You won't feel close to all of your teachers (and vice versa), but if spring of junior year comes around, and you have no teachers who know at least a little bit about your soul, that's bad, not because it looks bad to the colleges, but because you'll have missed a chance to grab on to life, give of yourself, and learn from the masters — and that kind of wisdom is simply too good to miss.

Chapter 31

LETTERS — THE NUTS AND BOLTS

As you think about the teachers who know you best, you also need to see if your colleges require letters from specific teachers. Most colleges will let you decide which teachers to choose, but some will ask for a letter from an English teacher, or a teacher you had in a class related to your major (engineering schools often ask for a letter from a math teacher, and art schools from an art teacher). It's good to have one letter from someone who can talk about your writing ability — that's often an English teacher, but it doesn't have to be (unless the college requires it).

If the college asks for two letters, sending three is usually OK (check the college's Web site), as long as you're pretty sure the third letter won't repeat what's in the other two. Students often send a third letter from a coach or a rabbi or a boss (or even a third teacher) that shows another side of the student, and that's great — as long as the ideas are fresh. But don't stretch it — it's pretty hard to justify sending four letters when two are asked for, and six are out of the question.

Once your letter writers give you the OK, thank them, and let them know when you'll need the letter. In some cases, you might have a September deadline, and a good letter takes about three weeks to prepare. By giving your writers plenty of time to prepare, you are giving them the respect they are due, and you are helping them to help you — that's why you ask in spring of the junior year.

If the colleges have recommendation forms your writers must complete (most letters are submitted online — see Chapter 32), fill out the top part of the forms with your name, etc. Give these forms to your letter writers at least three weeks before they're due — it's OK for them to submit the same letter to different colleges, but the forms are different, and need to be filled out individually. If your high school wants the letter writer to mail their letter directly to the college, give your writers envelopes addressed to the college with *two* stamps on them. This way, the writer completes the form, encloses the letter, and drops it in the mail …

… because you aren't supposed to see the letters. In asking for a letter of recommendation, you are asking a teacher to write a letter about you, not to write a letter to you. If this is a shock to you, get used to it; you'll soon fill out job applications where employers will want to talk to friends and former bosses without your knowing what they'll say.

While colleges will ask you (on the recommendation form) if you want to see the letters, you want to WAIVE that right. Experience tells me teachers generally write stronger letters if they know the student will never see it, and some colleges become suspicious if a student doesn't waive their right — why would a student ask for a letter from a teacher they don't trust? Since the only way you'll ever see the letter is after you're admitted, it's best to waive the right, and move on.

Be sure to send a thank you note to your writers once your application is in. In addition, follow up with your letter writers after you hear back from your colleges (whether you're admitted or not). You asked them to write a letter for you because they care about you, so they'll be curious to know how things worked out.

Chapter 32

APPLYING ONLINE AND USING COMMON APPLICATIONS

Most colleges have an online application that is usually easier to complete, sometimes less expensive to submit, and always easier for them to work with. Since most students can text faster than most adults can type, you probably won't haven any problems here — just watch out for two things:

"Save" versus "submit." Online apps let you work on part of the application, save that part, and come back to the app later — this way, you don't have to complete the entire application (including the essays) in one marathon session ...

... but here's the thing. Once you're done, and ready to turn the application in, be sure to hit Submit, NOT Save. Too many students hit Save out of habit, but that doesn't send your app to the admissions office; it just holds it in the incomplete application file. Once you're good to go, hit Submit, and look for an e-mail from the college in one or two days. If you don't get one, call them to make sure the application is there.

Making payment. Not everyone is crazy about paying for things online. Colleges respect that, so many allow you to mail in payment, or call it in ...

... just make sure to do it. Mom and Dad (and you) may get so caught up in the hoopla of submitting an application, you'll forget to send in the fee — and without the dough, your app won't go. Pay after you apply.

Other colleges let students use a Web site where you can apply to more than one college with the same application. The best known multi-college Web site is The Common Application, where over 450 colleges await your application.

These sites are great for students applying to several colleges — after all, how many times do you really want to fill out your name and address? Still, keep four things in mind so that the ease of a multi-college application doesn't become a nightmare on your street:

Each application has additional essays. These sites often let you submit the same first essay to every college, but most colleges will want more writing samples than that. Since these "supplemental essays" can add up quickly, make sure you know how much writing is required before you add extra colleges to your existing list — better yet, do some research on these colleges before you decided to apply "just for laughs."

Each application has its own payment. You may be filling out one application, but each college will still want a separate application fee. Just like the essays, these can add up; make sure you can afford to send that one app to so many colleges.

Get everyone's e-mail address right. Multi-college sites often ask for the e-mails of your counselor and letter writers — this way, they only have to fill out one form, too! This is very cool, as long as you have their correct e-mails; if not, your counselor and writers will never get their forms, and your app won't be finished. Double check their e-mails, and type them in slowly.

Be sure to waive your rights. We discussed this in Chapter 31, but it's really important to check the "I waive my rights to see my recommendations" box on a multi-college app, because once you answer this question, you can't change your mind, and that answer is submitted BEFORE you complete the application. If you answer incorrectly, you'll have to send a letter by US mail to every college, indicating you changed your mind — and if you have to do that, what's the point in applying online?

Chapter 33

THE BIGGEST HURDLE IS THE FIRST APPLICATION

The real challenge for a college counselor is how to help students whose first sense of application panic comes on a fall Saturday morning, when they bring a pen or laptop to the breakfast table, throw a last handful of Cocoa Doodles in their mouth, decide it's time to take on that first application — and they freeze on the line that says "Name."

In other words, they are coming out of the "College is Crazy" hype, and thinking about what they really want out of college for the first time in a long time, or for the first time ever.

I'm sorry I can't be at your breakfast table when there's nowhere to run to — if I could be there, I would tell you to go to your room.

Most students balk at filling out college applications because they view it as the first step towards leaving home. That's easy to see; this is the place where you listen to your music, text message long after your parents have gone to bed, and think about your life. The world outside has changed and challenged you, sometimes in ways you didn't like or didn't completely master — but you always had home to sort out what it all meant, and looked forward to what came next. Giving this place up won't be easy.

The good news is the colleges that are right for you will feel just like home. It may be in the dorm rooms, it may be at the library (hey, it happens), it may be the whole campus — but somewhere at those colleges, there is a spot waiting for you to reflect on the challenges of life, wonder about the possible, and text your BFFs til dawn. Once you think about college as your next home, completing the applications will be as easy as taking the written exam for your driver's license, because both are just the paperwork that leads to a greater sense of freedom. In the end, going to college isn't about leaving home — it's about taking home with you.

The second thing I would do is replace your earbuds with soundproof headphones. The application to a college a student loves often heads to the shredder when a well meaning neighbor asks, "Where is that college?," or Uncle Bob reports the college is nowhere to be found in the recently published rankings. If it turns out no other student at the local high school is applying to this college, this can become a trifecta for trauma.

When this happens, I encourage students to make the mature choice and be selfish. By fall, college-bound students know who they are and what they want in a college. Knowing what you know about college and yourself, it's important to keep the well-meaning insights of others in perspective — some may know you, some may know colleges, but very few (except your parents) will know both as well as you do. With self knowledge and college knowledge, everyone gets a best college, even if what's best for you is different than what's best for everyone else.

At this time of year, it's easy to think it's gonna take a miracle to get into college. You've worked too hard to believe in things that you don't understand — instead, remember what home means to you, stay focused on what you've learned about college and yourself, and your college applications will go flying out the door so quickly, you'll realize the miracle is you.

So pick up the pen, and pass the Cocoa Doodles. You can do this.

Chapter 34

CHANGING YOUR SCHEDULE —
DROPPING AP PHYSICS FOR HISTORY OF BADMINTON?
THINK AGAIN!

It's now the start of the school year — a new locker, a new schedule, and a new year — SENIOR year (woot!).

But wait. You've just looked at your schedule, and you're sure there's been a mistake. AP this; Advanced that; IB the other thing. This looks so hard, you're sure you won't have any fun this year — your SENIOR year (woot again!) ...

... so immediately, you go into the seven stages of grief.

Shock: Whoa! Look at this schedule!

Denial: Who put this schedule together? Not me!

Anger: This reeks! I'm not going to have time to do anything but study!

Bargaining: Wait — it's not too late to change my schedule. Maybe I can pick up some easier classes, like *Adele*, *Black Eyed Peas*, and *Chris Brown: The ABCs of Contemporary Music.*

Depression: But if I do that, I'll never get into college.

Testing: But maybe I can change a couple of classes and still be OK. Would that work?

Once you get to this stage, you should see your counselor — but first, ask yourself two questions:

- *If I drop this class, how strong is the rest of my schedule?*
  When colleges look at your senior year schedule, they'd like to see you taking the strongest classes you can possibly take that will challenge you. As you think about your class load,

how much homework you can handle, etc., remember that strength of schedule is considered the most important part of an application (along with grades) by virtually every college. If you're thinking about dropping your only advanced class (and colleges have a list of all the advanced classes your school offers), or if you're thinking about dropping this class in order to pick up a non-academic course, don't do anything until you talk to your counselor.

- **If I keep this class, will I be able to get good grades in my other classes?** In a perfect world, you should be taking the most demanding classes in every subject. However, if one demanding class is going to take up so much of your time that the grades in your other classes will suffer, a change may be the right thing to do. A B- in a sixth AP class won't really help all that much, if your grades in the other five classes dropped to Bs from As so you could work harder on getting the B- (I hope that makes sense.) Of course you should challenge yourself — but you don't want to drive yourself crazy, or hurt your chances of admission, either, and an academic plate that's too full can do both.

Whatever you decide here, remember — if you give a college a copy of your schedule, and then you change that schedule, _it is your responsibility to notify the college of that change immediately_. There are some students who believe that colleges don't care if you drop AP Chinese for AP Field Hockey — they do, and failing to tell colleges your schedule has changed can lead to a withdrawal of their offer of admission to you. So use your best judgment both before _and_ after you change your schedule.

The goal is to make senior year fun and challenging, but not impossible. That's not only the key to a rich life; it's the key to the best kind of college **acceptance** (woot, one more time)!

What does that mean, anyway?

One more thing — if you can't get all the challenging classes you want because they're offered at the same time, BE SURE to tell your counselor. They'll let the colleges know you're not slacking off.

Chapter 35

LINING UP AN INTERVIEW

While many colleges require letters of recommendation, far fewer require interviews. Most students breath a sigh of relief when they hear this, and I don't know why — after all, why wouldn't you want someone at the college of your dreams to hear about your dreams?

You can fulfill this requirement one of two ways. You can conduct an interview on campus — this is nice, because it means you'll have a chance to see campus as well, which is really a must before you attend a college. If you get an on-campus interview, it will most likely be with the person who will be reading your application, which is a plus.

The other way is through an interview with a graduate of the school, known hereafter as alumni. These interviews are usually local, so they can be built around your schedule. The alumni interviewers are trained by the college, so they know how to conduct an interview, and often offer some good insights into life at the college as a student, which are great to know.

If you want to interview on campus, you have to call the college — and most interview times fill up quickly (like by fall), so call in July. If the college requires an interview and you can't make it to campus, the local alumni will call you to set up the meeting. The meeting may be by in person or by phone; either one is fine.

If you come home and find a request for an interview on your voice mail **return the call within 24 hours**. Work out a time and date that works for both of you. If this is an in-person interview, you need to arrange a place to meet, which should be a public place that offers relative privacy (like a coffee shop). If it's a phone interview, arrange it so you'll be in a distraction-free room (no little brothers, parents or multi-tasking) and where you can use a land line, not a cell phone.

The day before the interview, confirm the date, time and place by calling either the college or the alumni. If you get voice mail, simply leave your name, the date, time and place where the meeting will occur, and a phone number where someone can call you if they have questions. This shows both courtesy and organization on your part — in general, colleges like both.

OK — now the big question — if it's face-to-face (or Skype), what to wear? Because this is an interview, and not a fashion show, you don't have to spend hours thinking about this — just look nice, and you'll be fine. For guys, this means a collared shirt and dark or khaki slacks and something other than sandals or sneakers; a few years ago, even liberal thinkers were telling guys not to wear earrings to interviews, but now some male interviewers wear them — so there's some room to negotiate here, but I'd leave them at home, and think about a tie.

For girls, this means a dressier, non-revealing top, slacks or a skirt (true confession here — I really think a skirt of knee length or longer leaves a better impression) and shoes that compliment the outfit. Having said all of this, I know many students who had great interviews in T-shirts and jeans — while I'm not recommending that, I point it out just to say this isn't the part of the interview to lose sleep over …

… and speaking of sleep, get lots the night before. *Risky Business* aside, interviews don't occur at parties, and good ones don't occur after parties.

Chapter 36

SHOWTIME

OK — so you've confirmed the appointment, and your mother likes what you're wearing. Good.

For a face-to-face interview, arrive for the interview early — at least five minutes ahead. This gives you a chance to catch your breath, get comfortable with where you'll interview, and a minute for the rest room if you need it. If you get lost on the way, CALL if you can. Being lost is not grounds for being denied admission; being gracious about getting lost is the thoughtful thing to do, and demonstrates your humanity to the interviewer. If the interviewer arrives after you do, stand up, say hello, smile, and offer your hand.

The key for all interviews is to just be yourself — really. The interviewer will probably ask you open-ended questions — questions where you will have to supply more than a "yes" or "no" answer. Typical questions are "Why are you interested in our college?" "What's the most interesting thing you've done?," or the famous, "Tell us about yourself." Your answers should be complete, and of a good length — about a minute or so. Keep the rules of a good college essay in mind — answer the question, show warmth, humor, intellect, and grace in your answers (easy on the humor — don't force a funny moment), and show your personal side without getting too personal. If you want to relate a story you told as part of your essay, that's fine, but don't make it the entire answer to a question — this is a chance to add to your application, not duplicate it.

If you're having an interview that isn't required, you've asked for the meeting — so now is the time to get down to business. If you want to talk about the unusual circumstances you've faced as a student (illness, family issues, boredom with school) and how you've overcome them, tell your story; if you've taken the tour and have additional questions (that you've written down in advance), fire away; if you're meeting to show interest in the college, talk about what makes you unique, where you think you want to go in life, and what you have to give to the college. The idea is to take charge while being gracious; to give the meeting substance without being lengthy, and to show the interviewer why the college can't exist without you. Keep these things in mind and you'll do well.

In all interviews, you'll be asked if you have any questions. It's good to think about one or two in advance — like the day before the interview. If you happen to think of one on the spot, that's great too — the advanced questions are just in case. These questions should require answers that aren't in the college catalog or brochure — remember, the quality of the question can show the thought and interest you've put in to investigating the college. You can also ask your alumni interviewer about their perceptions of the college; while the answer you get is just their perspective, it's still good information to have as you consider the best place to be.

When the face-to-face interview is over, stand up and shake hands; for all interviews, thank the interviewer, and off you go. It is exceptionally good form to call or e-mail the interviewer the next day to thank them for the interview, and invite them to please contact you if they have any other questions. I think it's a better idea to hand write a note, but the phone call or e-mail is my concession to modernity, and it still conveys a sense of gratitude most students don't extend.

Chapter 37
ESSAYS

I don't know why students freak about essays — they're all about YOU. Yes, this is the part where the show is all yours, where it's focused on Numero Uno, the Big Enchilada, the person you like so much, you put their reflection in the mirror every time you look into one.

That last one made ya think, didn't it?

That may sound selfish, but it's actually the key to writing an effective essay — be you. Most colleges give you a very general topic to write on, where you get to steer the ship; if the questions are specific, you answer them in a way that shows them who you are. Some ground rules:

- *Answer the question.* It's great to write a broad answer with lots of background, but if they want to know a person who inspired you, tell them. If you read your answer, and it's not clear to you who inspired you, the college will have no clue either — time to start over.

- *Answer the question honestly.* Don't say your father because you think it will move them, and don't say Sponge Bob just to be cute. The essay is a guided tour of your mind, life, vision, and soul — what you are, not what you think you're supposed to be. Show them the real deal.

- *Watch the humor.* An Ivy League rep once said if you could get him to laugh out loud while reading your application, you were in. Trouble is, lots of students try, and fail. What's funny to you may be dull, trite, pathetic, or strange to the committee. Try for warm and spirited — let Jane Lynch do shtick.

- *Watch the content.* Trite (an essay on deciding what the essay should be about) pathetic ("I'm not worthy — but take me anyway") or strange ("I'm really a vampire") are out.

Your writing should be an honest look at you, but this is an introduction, not the tenth week of therapy. Be focused and balanced, and you'll do fine.

- **Show it to an English teacher you like.** At least one friendly English teacher loves to slash essays with red pen — grammar, spelling, the whole tour. This is your new best friend; bring them your rough draft and chocolate, and let the games begin.

- **Write the essay yourself.** The essay is a guided tour of your life — as written by you. Having someone else do "significant editing" is your first act of college-level plagiarism, and it may be your last. Don't.

- **Repeat yourself.** You can use the same essay for different colleges, as long as the essay answers the question, and shows something about you. You'll need to take the names of other colleges out (Don't tell Brown "I've always wanted to go to Dartmouth"), and you want to put specifics in about the new college ("It's great that Chicago requires its students to swim. When I was six …"), but other than that, cut and copy away.

- **Write only on the weekends.** Weekdays are school, studying, and many extracurriculars; besides, essays written at 10 pm after three hours of homework are usually pretty bad. Aim to complete one set of essays each weekend, and you'll be in great shape.

Colleges would love to put you up for two weeks to really get to know every applicant — but if they did that, you'd be 45 before they admitted you. The essay takes the place of that two weeks — write it so that when they read it, they feel like you just left the room, and your chair is still warm.

Chapter 38

COLLEGE ESSAYS, PART 2:
THE 4 D'S COLLEGE REPS DON'T WANT TO HEAR,
AND MORE

Whenever I talk to college admissions officers — the people who actually read the essays you write — I ask them for advice to pass along to students. Year after year, they agree with what the last chapter told you; essays are the best chance for students to show who they are and what they sound like, and that's a key piece in the application process.

To my surprise, the reps also had some don'ts to pass along — things they see too many students include in their essays that just don't work well. I'm passing them along, so pay close attention — this is the kind of "special attention" you DON'T want your apps to get:

Avoid the Four Ds. Essays on negative life events can be very tricky. Unless enough time has passed since the experience, the essay can be too personal, too much of a rant, or just too hard to read. One rep said the general rule of thumb was no essays on the Four Ds — Drugs, Dating, Death and Divorce — but you get the idea. If you want to write about a personal challenge, emphasize what you learned and how you grew — if you dwell on the details, the essay will not achieve its purpose.

It's Not a Book Report. You may indeed think that *Zen and the Art of Motorcycle Maintenance* was the best book ever written, but there's a point where your analysis of the book becomes more academic (and about the book) than personal (and about you). If you're writing about your response to the book or how it influenced your life, the right writing ratio is a lot less about the book and way more about your life — in this case, it really is all about you.

Grandma Barbara Isn't Going to College. "Less is more" is also the case if you're asked to write about someone who's had an impact on your life. It's great you love that your hero was born in Scotland and learned the bagpipes at age four, but that level of detail leaves less words for the college to hear about what you've done with the inspiration that special someone has given you — and it's that story they want to hear.

It's OK to go on and on about Granny B if she's applying to college, too; if she isn't, a few specifics and a summary of qualities will nicely set the stage for what you think about all she's done, and ways she's made a difference in your view and interactions with the world. That's the main entrée on the menu of the college essay — let the reps dig in to a generous portion.

Don't Forget — Additional Information is a Beautiful Thing. One rep pointed out that most applications have a space where students can add details to their application the college needs to know. The Additional Information box lets you talk about when you were ill in 10th grade, when you moved in the middle of junior year, why a summer school grade is still incomplete, and more.

Good Essays are Like Good Cheese — Let Them Age. Once you're done with an app, hit Save and let it sit for two days; that way, you can use the extra box to add the things you remember at four in the morning, then hit Submit with confidence — your full story is told.

Chapter 39

ESSAYS, PART 3:
OVERCOMING TWO CHALLENGES

Essay questions can change from year to year and from college to college, but one that often comes up is, "Describe a challenge you have faced and how you overcame it."

If this topic seems like a challenge itself, keep these basic ideas in mind:

- **The goal of the essay is for colleges to learn more about you.** Essays are the opportunity to show a college the person behind the grades and test scores. Effective essays tell them a story, give them a taste of your voice and a peek at the way you look at the world, and show them your ability to write.

- **A challenge isn't always a crisis.** A "setback" or "adversity" can include a serious situation, but challenges aren't always life-threatening as much as they are life-jarring, or life-changing. Wake-up calls come in different ringtones — talk about one that authentically got you thinking, and you'll be fine.

- **Some challenges may be too personal.** Generally speaking, boyfriend/girlfriend breakups are out — try as you might, most students can't write about these without sounding too abandoned or too bitter. The same is usually true for challenges with addictions; you are moving on beautifully with your life, but talking about the experience is usually the last skill you gain. It's always a good idea to show your essays to a counselor; if you're writing about something very personal, a counselor review is a must.

- **And one is just too cheesy.** No matter what, do NOT use this topic to address "the challenge I overcame in writing my answer to this question." This is a variation of writing an essay about writing an essay; it's rarely authentic, and college reps read way more of these than they'd like — because when they've read one, that's one too many. This approach almost always comes off as an "I love me" message — is that really what you want to say to colleges?

- **Don't skimp on the resolution and reflection.** It's good to give a clear picture of what you were facing, but dwelling too long on the problem doesn't show the college how you resolved it, or what you think about the experience now that it's behind you (or if it's behind you.) Colleges want to hear about an important life lesson you've experienced, and the finale is more important than the overture — make sure you create balance.

- **Like all essays, write this one yourself.** Too much "help" on an essay makes a college suspicious, and leaves you with nowhere to go next fall. Talk about adversity.

The other challenge is when an essay asks for a minimum number of words, but no maximum. The challenge to overcome now is that you will overwrite, something that is very easy to do for most students. Minimums offer you the temptation to just keep writing, until you finally start talking about your Aunt Eve's summer trip to Niagara Falls, and you realize maybe it's time to stop.

The key to avoiding this temptation is to do what I've always urged you to do — show your essays to an English teacher who loves you. This careful mix of expertise and compassion will allow them to brandish the red pen with affection, precision, and empathy, allowing you to tell the colleges what they need to know without pushing them to the point of boredom, madness, or worse — tedium. English teachers are busy people, so ask them ahead of time, set up an appointment, and bring armloads of chocolate.

Yes, I did say armloads.

Chapter 40

THE FINAL CHECK

With the essays written, you're in the home stretch. A few final touches:

- Almost every college has a secondary school report form, asking for an official transcript and/or counselor comments. If you gave an online app your counselor's e-mail, cool; if not, these forms go to your counselor AT LEAST a month before they are due. Check to see what your school's policy is, then fill out the top and hand them in. If the college wants your grades from the first half of senior year, turn that form in as well.

- I'm hoping you checked your transcript for incorrect or missing grades when you met with your counselor in February. If not, check now — nothing ruins an application like a D in Calculus you never got.

- Use your resources wisely. It's good news if an app's due January 1st, (you can work on it over break), but your counselor won't be in the office December 28th, so make sure you have all the info you need from school on the last day of school. ATTENTION ALL STUDENTS: Even if you have access to your counselor's home number, don't call them. They love you, but the absence of your planning isn't their emergency. Unless they tell you otherwise, make your best guess, send it in, then see if your counselor needs to help you fix it the first day back.

- Have someone look over your application to make sure it's complete. You can earn big "sweetie" points if you let your parents do this during your weekly meeting — but they are checking the form you completed, not filling it out for you.

- If the college requires official test scores and you haven't sent them, go to *www.collegeboard.org* (SATs) or *www.act.org* (ACT) and order them *now*.

- If one of the college's essays was, "Why us?," stop and read your answer very carefully. This essay usually has a very small maximum (150 words), so most students blow it off — and that's a big mistake. You answer here shows if you did your homework on this college, and you really know what makes it special to you. If the answer you wrote describes any other college, go back and re-write it — it matters that much.

If you're mailing out apps two days or less from the deadline (online apps are better), go to the post office and watch them get postmarked (bring the MP3 player along — the line is serpentine in December).

After a day (or five) of resting from application frenzy, it's time to rejoin the living. Waiting to hear from a college is like waiting to be asked out on a date — the more you stay home, the longer until the phone rings. It's the last six months of senior year, so there has to be something on the "to do" list you're dying to get to — get busy.

In addition, don't look back. As a 9th grader, you wanted perfect grades, smoked SATs, universal acclaim as The Ruler of Community Service, and an admissions letter from Harvard engraved in gold. Maybe you got those things, maybe you didn't; either way, if the last app goes in the mail and you've done everything you can to make it all work, there's nothing else that can be added — except keep living a rich, full life.

P.S. If a college says they're missing something, don't freak — contact the right person (teacher, counselor, yourself) and send it in immediately. Forms gets lost, but it's OK; you're getting a do-over. Send it in, and move on.

Chapter 41
SECOND GUESSING YOUR LIST? GUESS AGAIN

Late October can be the hardest time for applying to colleges. You've already submitted a couple of applications, and now you're up to your Uggs in essays and deadlines for more colleges. You're starting to wonder if this is all really worth it, when along comes a thick envelope from one of the colleges you applied to in September — congratulations, you're in!

You have now entered the Goldilocks zone. (Forgot about her? Go to *http://www.dltk-teach.com/rhymes/goldilocks_story.htm* — DON'T ask your English teacher, who will tell you the story is a metaphor of global consumption by Western civilization.)

Why Goldilocks? Right now, you think your college list is:

Too hard. With five class papers to do and the fall play, you're sure you are applying to too many colleges. You only visited half of them, the time you spend on essays would be much better spent on keeping your grades up, and you're already admitted to one college — do you really need more?

Too soft. Sure, you're in at one college — but that was a safety school. In fact, every school you're applying to looks like a sure thing. Maybe it's time to ramp things up — and if that means more essays, you can take your laptop to Grandma's on Thanksgiving.

These may seem to be opposites, but they are signs of the same thing — you are stressed about the application process. Pull up a bowl of porridge, and let's sort this out with three simple questions:

How did you feel about your college list in September? If you put a lot of thought into your choices, visited some campuses and researched the others, chances are you'd be cutting out some options by cutting down on the list; the busy-ness of school is blocking your view of the big picture, and it's time to take a breath.

However, if you threw the list together to get Mom and Dad off your back, you may now have a better idea of what you want — or don't want. If that's the case, there's time to re-visit the list, and a good reason to do so.

How many essays do you really have left? Count up the college essays you have to answer. Now, divide that number by six. That's the number you have to complete each weekend to finish the apps by mid-December. If you mix and match short and long essays, you're probably OK if you have to do three each weekend, maybe four. (Remember, no writing during the week. That's time for school work, which is the way you keep your grades up.)

Then again, if you have to write something like one-sixth of an essay each weekend, you have room to apply to more colleges. Write down what you're looking for in a college, and spend this weekend looking around for more; it sounds like you can skip the essays for a while.

Have your college goals changed since September? If you have new college plans, a review of your list is the right thing to do. If you really know all of the colleges are keepers, it's time to pull up your socks and do the heavy lifting of the essays. Persisting now will be good practice for college, when you have to choose between turning a paper in on time, and the Euchre tournament.

Goldilocks made bad choices — trespassing, destruction of private property, and napping after a big meal. Don't let this happen to you; step back, think about what matters most to you, and you'll make a decision about college apps that's just right.

Chapter 42

MAKING IT THROUGH HOLIDAY BREAKS WITHOUT BEING BROKEN

Completing college applications can be hard work, work that often runs through the holiday season. Since everyone else is taking some time off, this would seem to be the perfect opportunity to hang out with your family, especially since this could be your last Thanksgiving/New Year/Kwanzmasakah as a full-time occupant of your parents' home. How could this possibly be a bad idea?

"Hombre," says you, "you clearly don't know my parents, or my Uncle Bob."

Amgios and amigas, it's time for a siesta. Here are the three keys to thriving (not just surviving) this holiday season:

Treat Uncle Bob Like You, and He, Are Adults. If you're smart enough to go to college, you're smart enough to sort out how Uncle Bob operates — and that's the key to success. Once he's through updating you on his thriving business and gloating about the political party of his choice, he's going to put a large piece of turkey on his fork, and ask, "So, how's the college hunt going?"

You're now thinking this is the end. You haven't heard from the college that was supposed to decide in October, and your other colleges are small schools Uncle Bob hasn't heard of — heck, *you* hadn't even heard of them until last year.

And this, my friend, makes for a wonderful foundation for your response.

"Well, Uncle Bob, I applied to Eastnorthern State U, and thought of you when I answered the essays, since you've told me how much you love the school. I guess everybody's uncle feels that way, because the college is weeks behind in admissions decisions, but I should hear by Super Bowl.

"I know Mom has told you about my other schools, where some of the students major in the History of Haiku and take classes like Fruit Leather in a Modern Society. I won't hear from them until spring, but if I decide to attend one of them, I'll be sure to bring a flare gun with me to campus, in case they try to force feed me with tofu."

At this point, Uncle Bob will look at you, chuckle a little, and then go back to talking about the glory, or evils, of Ronald Wilson Reagan.

Welcome to adulthood.

Your Applications and Black Saturday. The next holiday hurdle is the Saturday after Thanksgiving (or Christmas or …) when even the adults are ready for a break from each other. This is typically the time when your parents — who love you — will say, "Honey, Uncle Bob is going out to lunch with us. Don't you think this would be a good time to work on your college essays?"

This requires preparation. You put together a spreadsheet ahead of time with the name of every college you're applying to, the date each application is due, and the date you will work on that application. Print out a copy and keep it in your back pocket, saving it for this moment, when you open it with a modest flourish, hand it to your parents, and say; "I've got it covered. Have a great lunch."

And as you put your earphones back on to fall under the spell of Justin Gaga, you will see your parents weep with amazement and joy. Their widdle baby is all growed up.

Remember the Reason for the Season. You have parents who love you, an Uncle Bob who is the loveable kind of crazy, and a world of possibilities awaiting you in college. If ever there was a time for gratitude, it is now.

Ariba.

Chapter 43

SCHOLARSHIP ESSAYS IN 600 WORDS OR LESS

How are you doing, senior? Back at school now, right? Had a good holiday? Cool!

So — ready to write some more?

Yeah, yeah — I figured you'd say that. The keyboard calluses from your application essays are finally beginning to fade, and along comes me to remind you of an essential point — you still can't go to college if you don't have the money.

So it's time to do some scholarship essays.

Unlike looking for a college, this hunt is really pretty easy. First, go back to *www.finaid.org* and look for scholarships that meet your interests, talents and backgrounds. Your school counselor may have a different site they like more, or a neighbor may have found college cash somewhere else, so ask and look around.

Next, scope out your high school counseling Web site or ask your counselor about the list of local scholarships that are available. This is the most neglected source of scholarship money, because most people think the $200 or $500 scholarships from the local VFW or the Kiwanis club aren't all that big. Fair enough — but if it takes an hour to write an essay for a $200 scholarship, that means you're making the same hourly rate as a first-year lawyer, and you're way younger.

In addition, remember that local scholarships have a smaller pool of applicants. Anything you find on finaid.org is being seen by tens of thousands of eyes; if you're in the only high school in town, how many students are really going to apply for the Good Citizen scholarship?

Once you hit these sites, look for scholarships that evolve around the same theme. A number of scholarships center on patriotism. This increases the chances that you can write one well done essay on, say,

America's future, apply most of it to six or seven essays, and be a serious contender for each one. Suppose 3 of those scholarships come your way — you're now up to $600 an hour.

You'll also want to ask your counselor if you can fill out one application for all of the local scholarships. Counselors know it's a pain to complete so many scholarship applications (and the VFW gets discouraged if only 3 kids apply for their scholarship), so they create one application for all local scholarships. You fill out one app, make enough copies for each scholarship, write a specific essay for each one, and, *voila*!

Another *magnifique* option is to use what you wrote in your college essays in your scholarship essays. It's more than OK to do this IF the college essay answers the scholarship question — if not, it's still a good way to get some ideas for scholarship topics.

The last "paying for college" thing you'll want to do (you've already complete the FAFSA, right?) is take one more look at your college list. This was covered in Chapter 21, but if you haven't done so, now is the time.

It's way too easy to get caught up in admit letters in April that come with financial aid packages where four years of loans will cost more than a Volt — but instead of being shocked, you'll say, "Oh, this is just too wonderful. I'll find a way to pay for it."

It's certainly true that things can work out in amazing ways, but when your college payment options boil down to starting out your work life with a car payment-sized student loan or hitting the Power Ball, filling out one more college app now creates a Door #3 that could seem like a deal come April.

And it probably doesn't require an essay.

Chapter 44

I LOVE YOU, YOU'RE PERFECT — NOW GO STUDY

It may seem mighty early, but grumblings are emerging in the past few years about seniors slacking off in their studies as early as January. Known as "senioritis", this mental vacation doesn't usually happen until April, when the sun is out, graduation is in sight, and a young person's fancy turns to — well, not school.

I've long thought senioritis was vastly misunderstood — it's not that you don't care about learning, as much as you need a break from thinking, writing, and waiting to hear from, college. Add in a little holiday stress from relatives asking about college plans, and you're simply whipped. What you need now more than anything else is a little understanding, a few words of encouragement …

… and a kick in the flash drive.

I know, I know — I'm supposed to be the understanding counselor. Truth is, I am; I'm understanding that students are getting more deferrals than ever before, where colleges are asking students for grades in the classes they're currently taking, and keeping a VERY close eye on the grades you'll earn in your last semester of high school. With increases in applications, more students are applying for the same number of seats at many colleges, and even a few less seats in colleges that are facing tough financial times. This means colleges are getting more students with higher grades, so they can take a closer look, and ask for more information.

I get that you want to stay in vacation mode, and I get that this is your last Winter concert, spring sports season, prom. I also get that the grades you get may be the difference in the offers of admission you get, or get to keep- get it?

Going to cruise control right now is like saying the four-foot putt doesn't matter, since you've already hit the ball 400 yards. Phil Mickelson knows best — if it ain't in the hole, the match isn't yours.

So enjoy these rites of your last year in high school, but also do what you need to do — pull out the viewbook of Dream School U to remember your goal, paint your nails with highlighter yellow, have your mother hide QBox12000 until you've studied for two hours each night — and get the job done.

Your applications show colleges the student you've been, and many are asking to see if that's the student you still are. The answer they get isn't blowing in the wind; it's going to be written in the essay of the life you live from now until June, while you keep your student skills sharp, continue to contribute to the community you're in now, and learn a few things that will make the transition to college a smooth one ...

... which includes a demanding schedule. There is a temptation right about now to change your schedule and make it less rigorous. Please remember — if you've given a college a list of your senior year classes, and that list changes significantly, you are obligated to write them and explain why. Sometimes the reasons are understandable (class conflict), but sometimes they aren't — and colleges want to know that.

If you have a significant change, you have to let them know. If you're making your schedule harder, you don't have to tell them, but you should — I mean, don't you want them to know you're taking your game to the next level?

No, no — I mean your academic game, not *World of Mariocraft 12*.

Chapter 45

A WORD ABOUT GRADE GRUBBING: NO

In addition to thinking about changing their spring schedules, many seniors will be getting second semester or trimester grades and realize the time they spent at the Harry Potter film festival and a hint of Thanksgiving senioritis have taken their toll on last semester's grades:

"A B+ in Physics?" "A C in Business Law?" "A *WHAT* in English?"

Welcome to grade groveling season, the time of year when parents across America look at their senior's laundry and say, "What are these stains on the knees of these pants, and how did they get there?"

From buttering-up to begging, from outrage to despair, seniors will spend the next couple of weeks planning, scheming, and hoping that they can squeeze just one little grade bump from three or four teachers, largely because they are certain colleges will take one look at these grades and say, "Yeah, well, no."

I suppose this is where I'm supposed to offer words of solace and encouragement, and outline some approaches towards importunacy that will succeed. OK, here goes:

Good luck with that.

I know you feel badly, much like the point guard who sinks the winning shot after the buzzer sounds, or the junior who finally understands the writing prompt on the ACT on their drive home from the test center. This isn't easy to live with, and you were so close, but it just didn't happen.

"But, Sensei," says you, "college is on the line, and I can fix this, because time hasn't run out. I'm still in high school, and I still have the same teacher."

True enough, young grasshopper — but look at the calendar, and see who's behind. It's second sem/trimester, and that grade was for first sem/trimester. On the time-space continuum, the jig is up — and if you don't understand that, maybe you really did deserve that low Physics grade. Just sayin'.

If that's not enough to get your head out of the rear-view mirror, remember that a small bump in one class grade — say, from a B+ to a B — raises your GPA by about .008. Combine that with the advice a college rep gave me — "one grade alone will never sink a student" — and I'd say it's time to leave your teachers in peace …

… which leads to my last point. Unlike Aunt Midge's socks, grades aren't gifts given by someone else — they are earned by you. If you have reason to believe your grade was calculated incorrectly, follow the grade appeal process outlined in your school handbook.

At the same time, I'm guessing this process has nothing to do with baking cookies for your teacher, following them to the parking lot at the end of the day , or having your parents "accidentally" bump into them at the grocery store — and it really doesn't involve saying "but a grade this low will keep me out of college."

From what I know, that's not true, and even if it is, the person who gave you this "gift" of a grade isn't looking at you from the teacher's desk third period.

They're looking at you in the bathroom mirror every morning.

Believe me when I tell you, I'm feelin' it for ya, but it's time to pull up those socks Aunt Midge bought you and move on…

…because one low grade last sem/trimester may not keep you from being admitted, but a couple of low grades in your final sem/trimester can put you on the fast track to admissions offer take-back.

There's nothing you can do if you fell behind, so now it's time to spring ahead.

Chapter 46
20-MINUTE MEETINGS, TO BE CONTINUED

To review the last few chapters: There is no letting up on taking tough classes; no giving up on writing essays; no slacking off on homework, and no telling the teachers how smart they are in the hopes they'll change last semester's B to an A.

Fair enough, you think. At least you can stop meeting with your parents each week, now that the college choices are all made.

Yes. About that.

It would seem something has happened since you first carved 20 minutes out of every week to talk with your parents about college. To begin with, they've learned to give you your space; most parents think I am crazy to limit them to 20 minutes of college talk a week, especially during the weeks in the fall when you were working on applications and telling them absolutely nothing beyond their allotted time. They learned to trust you more, which will come in handy over time — like when you go to college, buy your first couch, and name your child after a Klingon god.

But something else has happened. Because you met each week when no one was rushing to get you anywhere, your parents had a chance to really see what you've made of yourself since the last time things weren't so crazy — which for most families, is when you were about four. I have to tell you; they really liked what they saw. And they'd like to keep seeing it, every week, for about 20 minutes.

This probably makes no sense to you, but when you came home and said "Last winter exam. Yes!," they said, "Last winter exam. NO!" They told you they cried at this year's Sadie Hawkins Dance because of how nice you looked, right? Nope — last one. And remember they once dreaded having you home with them for a snow day? They were screaming for joy right along with you this year, weren't they?

Through the 20 minute meetings, your parents have realized they have a child who is smart, knows who they are, and understands a little about how the world works — and that child is moving out of their house in less than six months. Giving you up then is something they'll figure out; giving you up now is something they'd just as soon not do, just not yet.

Of course, you don't have to talk about college — now is not the time to sit together in the living room, holding hands and listening to the cuckoo clock chirp away the hours until college decisions arrive. Go out and eat, catch a movie, go bowling, wait in line together for tickets for the Justin Bieber nostalgia tour — but go do something.

Love is as much a verb as it is a noun, and showing them what you feel in a time of uncertainty (for both you and them) can make a memory that will last far longer that whatever East Coast U has to say in a couple of weeks.

No college decision will change how they feel about you, just like it shouldn't change how you feel about yourself. Twenty weekly minutes of together time that isn't "required" will bring that point home as nothing else can, and build a stronger base for whatever is waiting after Decision Day.

Give it some thought, while you go work on your next scholarship essay. They're sure thinking about it — they told me as much.

(Nice eye roll, by the way. Did you tell the colleges you can make them go in different directions like that while sighing like a leaky steam valve?)

Chapter 47
UNDERSTANDING FINANCIAL AID AWARDS

We're talking about financial aid awards before we talk about admissions decisions because things can get a little crazy when colleges start telling you if you're in — so we need to plan ahead.

Award letters can be a little dense, and no two are structured the same way, so comparing apples to apples can be challenging. Since paying for a college education is like buying a new car every year for four consecutive years, understanding what you're getting into is a must. Here's how:

- **Read the financial aid award letter five times.** You heart is racing because you're going to follow your parent's footsteps to East Coast College, you (or your parents) have skimmed the award letter twice, and you think you can afford to pay most of what you believe the letter says you'll have to pay. Not good enough.

  Skimming is great, but put the letter away, do the Steve Martin dance for five hours, then pick up the letter again that night, and read it again — then again the next morning, and again over the weekend. If the letter tells you different things at different times, you do not fully understand it. That's pretty typical, but it still isn't good.

- **Use the tools.** Colleges often send along worksheets with the letter; some have more information on the Web, and others simply say "Call us." This is no time not to ask for directions; use the financial GPS accessories to learn where you are, and where you think your bank account is heading.

- **Call anyway.** Even if you SWEAR you know what the letter says, use the expertise of the financial aid office to your advantage. If you don't know what to say, try this: "We received my (my child's) acceptance letter, and we're so thrilled about their getting in, I'm not sure I can completely focus on the award letter. As I read it, they'll receive five thousand in grant we don't have to pay back, they'll work 8 hours a week at an on-campus job, and there's twelve hundred dollars in student loans. Is that right?"

- *As Elmer Fudd would say, be vewwy vewwy quiet.* Once you tell the financial aid office what you see, let them talk. It's not uncommon for aid officers to bring up your child's file and find a better way to package the aid, or discover new money that's just become available. They are good at their job, and they want to help you — listen, and let them.

- *Update them.* Your financial picture may have changed dramatically since you filled out the forms two months ago — it happens all the time. Be sure the college knows this, and be ready to send documentation to support your claims. Nothing may change, but the only way something good might happen is if you tell them.

Chapter 48

THE CHAPTER TO READ ON MARCH 15ᵀᴴ

If you've taken any of the last few chapters to heart, what could
have been a winter of discontent waiting to hear from the colleges
has instead been filled with writing thoughtful scholarship essays,
recommitting your energies to learning, and rediscovering your parents
are great people.

But now the winter is past, and the voice of the college admissions
offices is heard in our land.

I understand this is a time of great excitement and anxiety for almost all
of you, but before we go any further, you must understand three things
about selective college admissions. I cannot stress the importance of
reading this thoroughly, twice, before you move ahead — OK?

1. There is an excellent chance applications to all colleges will be
   at an all-time high. The number of US high school graduates
   is slated to go down for the next 10 years, but applications
   to college are expected to rise. This means getting admitted
   to highly selective colleges is more difficult than ever before,
   simply because of the number of students that have applied.
   Of course, other factors enter into the admissions process
   — grades, letters of recommendation, test scores, etc. — but
   since most students who apply to these colleges academically
   qualify for admission, an increase in the number of applications
   makes admission that much harder.

2. There is a common reason why colleges deny admission to
   students. The number one reason selective colleges deny
   admission to students is simple — they run out of room. If
   they had more dorm rooms, and more professors, and more
   classrooms, they'd *love* to take more students — but they
   cannot do justice to the students they do admit by taking too
   many, since no one gets a quality education that way — and
   that's not fair to anyone.

3. An admissions decision is NOT a character indictment. With
    more applications, and limited space, colleges must create
    a learning community that is exciting, diverse, and rich with
    opportunities. How colleges do that is a combination of art
    and science, a mixture of data (grades and test scores) and
    insight (personal statements, letters of recommendation,
    etc.), and, frankly, a little guesswork. In deciding who gets
    admitted, these selective colleges will tell you that just about
    everyone who decides to apply to a selective college qualifies
    for admission — they would be a great student, benefit
    the college tremendously, and contribute to the college in
    many ways. Since you applied to a selective college, those
    compliments would apply to you.

    Given that, I can't think of any way a letter of denial or waitlist
    should be interpreted to mean "The college doesn't like me",
    or worse "I am not a good person". College admissions is
    about many things, but it is never a judgment about you as a
    person, or about everything you have accomplished.

    Most colleges go to great pains to point this out when they
    send their denial letters. Believe me when I tell you that they
    aren't just being nice; they truly respect and honor everything
    you have done as a student and as a person, and they are
    grateful you applied to their college. That might not mean
    much the minute you open the letter, but I hope it will over
    time — whether the college says yes, no, or maybe, your
    value and worth as a person is cast in stone, and can be shaken
    by absolutely no one, be it another person, or an admissions
    committee.

Your life isn't in that envelope or e-mail; your admissions decision is.
You already have a life, and a fine one at that.

Chapter 49

THE BEST ADVICE WHEN A COLLEGE SAYS NO

The real Madness of March has nothing to do with basketball — it starts when colleges announce their admissions decisions, usually around March 20th. As a pre-game warm-up, let's review what we know:

- Most selective colleges report an increase in applications every year.
- Since these schools don't admit more students, that means they'll be saying no to more students ...
- ... and wait-listing more students. This increase means fewer students will be admitted from the wait list come May — and if they are admitted, financial aid will be scarce.

To ease your concerns, I have one word of advice. OK, it's actually a number.

850.

To begin with, calm down. This is not the high score on some new version of the SAT. Eight hundred, fifty is the number of valedictorians recently rejected from one of America's most prestigious colleges. These students represented the best in their high schools; they did everything they were "supposed" to do — and yet, they didn't even get to the wait list.

At this point, you're probably thinking one of two things:

1. *"Wow, they put in all of that work for nothing."*
2. *"Geez, if they can't get in, I don't stand a chance."*

First things first. It had to be hard to be turned down by a school they loved — but did all of that preparation really lead to nothing? Given everything these students had learned, the many ways they had grown, and how they overcame adversity and embraced creativity in making Plans B, C, and Q, did they really get nothing out of it?

If so, they have every right to be unhappy, but not with the college. They should be unhappy for letting the sun rise and set 1307 times from the first day of 9th grade to the day the college said no, never once appreciating all that each of those days had to offer in and of themselves.

They should hang their heads a little to realize, just now, the difference they've made to their classmates, their teammates, and the people they served in the soup kitchen.

And if they look back with a little regret on the many times they blew off a compliment from a parent or a teacher because the goal of college wasn't realized just yet, that's more than OK. They now know it was at that moment that the goal of fully living each day was conquered with a flourish — and understanding that will make each day all the richer at the wonderful college that had the good sense (and room) to take them.

What about the colleges you've applied to? They're looking for great students who have done wonderful things with their lives, and will work nicely with the other students that are coming to campus. That blend goes beyond test scores and class rank — it goes to who you are, what you care about, and how you see the world. Problem is, they run out of room before they run out of highly qualified applicants.

The thing to focus on then, is not who told you no, but who told you yes. If a college wants you but runs out of room, that's their fault; if they don't see you for who you really are, well, maybe that's not the place for you after all. Either way, your contributions will be greatly admired, and badly needed, by the college that has the good sense to tell you yes — which means any no, from any college, simply cannot touch you.

Chapter 5Ø
THREE KINDS OF DECISIONS

When you hear from a college, you'll get one of four decisions:

Admission. Also known as the "thick" envelope, the offer of admissions includes information on housing, orientation, and financial aid. Be sure to read all of it; this information will be of great value to you if you need to decide among several offers of admission.

Conditional Admission. Colleges offer you a seat in the freshman class with a requirement — generally, that you participate in a tutoring or student support program, that your first semester grades are at a certain level, or that you come to campus over the summer to participate in a college readiness program. These offers of admission are not an "either/or" proposition — if you want to go to that college, you must satisfy the requirements outlined in the offer of admission.

Not Offered Admission. News that a college cannot offer you admission usually comes in a thin envelope. As I said before, colleges mean it when they say they wish they could offer you admission, and they value your work as a student; it's just that colleges simply run out of room. As I also said before, admissions decisions aren't a judgment on your life — they just can't take everyone.

I'm sometimes asked if an admissions decision can be appealed. Just like every college handles admissions decisions differently, every college handles appeals differently — and remember, colleges do not have to offer any kind of appeal at all. In general, follow these guidelines:

Read your letter closely. These letters often explain both the procedures you need to follow to file an appeal, and the things colleges look for in reviewing an appeal. If your letter gives you no indication, call the office of admission and ask what their appeal policy is — and remember that some colleges will not take appeals except (or even) in very rare circumstances.

See if you can find out why you were denied admission in the first place. A conversation with an admissions officer may give the college enough additional information about you to form the basis of an appeal. If the college needs more information, you can ask for details on what the college would like to see — or, in some cases, you can find out if an appeal would not be the best use of your time.

Generally speaking, colleges will look at an appeal closely if you can provide additional information above and beyond what you included in your original application that shows you are a strong and/or unique student. Seventh semester grades, progress reports from your current classes, additional letters of recommendation, a supporting paragraph or two from your counselor, previously unexplained circumstances — these kinds of things can make a difference.

Remember that a successful appeal depends on a variety of factors — your strength as a student, what you've been doing with your life since you applied (see?), your continued interest in the college, the number of spaces the college has available, etc. In some cases, continued interest and strong grades may be enough to get you in on appeal — but in some cases, it won't.

An appeal isn't a sure thing, and the extra energy it requires to put an appeal together — not just yours, but the energy of your counselor, your teachers, and the college — can be high at this busy time of year. Before you start an appeal, be sure to think about your chances of success, and your real interest in the college, and let your answers guide you accordingly.

Those are the three simple possibilities. The toughie comes next.

Chapter 51
WAITLISTS

A letter indicating you've been waitlisted usually comes all by itself. The letter indicates that the college is still considering your application, but must hear from the admitted students first before they may — again, that's may — offer you admission.

This is tricky for two reasons. First, it's tough to wait longer; you were ready to hear yes or no, and you got "give us a little longer." Many students just can't live with the uncertainty anymore; if that's you, thank the college, say you're not interested, and move on.

Second, waitlist rules vary greatly by college — so ...

- Re-read the letter from the college to see if it gives you any information about the wait-list — how the order is determined, when it is determined, and what you need to do to stay on it. If all of the admitted soccer players turn down College X and College Y, College X may go to the waitlist only for soccer players, whereas College Y may simply start offering admission to the students at the top of the list, whether they play soccer or not (and risk a lousy season). Find out if you're dealing with an X or Y.

- If this information isn't in the letter, call the college and ask. They may give you some suggestions; if they do, write them down, since they are basically telling you how to improve your chances of moving up on the list.

Next, it's decision time. Given the college options you have, do you still feel it's worth pursuing this college as a possible option? As you think about this, it's **very** important to ask two questions —

1. If a slot doesn't open up at this college, what college will I select?

2. If a slot does open up at this college, what college will I select?

If the answer to these questions is the same, you're done here — move on. If your decision depends in part on financial aid, remember that the amount of aid available to students who come off the waitlist is usually limited. Colleges offer all of their aid to admitted students first; as a result, the aid available to waitlisted students is limited to the amount of aid turned down by admitted students. That's no reason to pack it in — it's just something to consider, or ask about.

If you decide to go for it, don't be shy. "I want you to know I am still very interested in attending College X this fall" sends a clear statement of where you stand; if College X is your first choice, you can say that, too (but remember only one first choice.) Grades in current classes, additional awards and activities, maybe another letter — all of that may help, but don't drive them crazy, and tell the truth. Send in one complete packet of new material as soon as it's ready, then call or e-mail about two weeks after that.

Most colleges won't review their waitlist until after May 1st, which is when students are expected to notify one — and only one — college they'll be going there in the fall. If you're still waiting to hear from a waitlisted college on April 30th, put in the required May 1st deposit at another school. If the college of your dreams pulls you off the waitlist later, cancel your admission at the other college in writing — and know you probably won't get your deposit back.

If you want to go for it, give it your all — but remember, you have a life; what you're looking for is a college.

Chapter 52
WAITING FOR A YEAR

Tell me the truth — when I told you to apply to six to 10 colleges, you thought I was out. Now it's late April of your senior year, and Chapter 21 has set in — you're not sure what to do.

Right about now, some students think about putting college on hold. This is pretty common, and choosing to defer — right, the same word used when colleges ask for more time — has its advantages. Students who defer get the chance to do something they've always wanted to do — see the world, work with the poor, study a language, earn more scratch for college, or maybe just chill.

Parents often freak about this choice; they're convinced that once you're out, you won't come back. Colleges don't feel that way — in fact, most colleges let you take a year off, and automatically hold a spot for you for the following fall, so long as you ask for a deferral before May 1st of your senior year, and promise not to take classes somewhere else. Not every college does this, so be sure to ask; since I teach college courses, I can tell you that students who take a year off usually come back more focused on school and eager to learn.

If you think deferral (also known as a "gap year") might be for you, apply to colleges as if you weren't going to defer — the logistics of applying to college are *huge* once you're out of high school. It's better to make a plan for next year while you're still in high school, whether it includes college or not — and "no college" is a good choice, if it's for the right reason, but you want to keep your options open.

"Fair enough" says you, "but where can I get some ideas about what to do?"

A number of Web sites can help you fill in the important details in planning a gap year. Some, like Rustic Pathways and Where There be Dragons offer travel and study programs abroad, while other programs like Dynamy give students internships to understand more about their personal and career interests. Many ideas can be found on gap year sites, but make sure the company is credible before you work with them. Also, many of these programs can be pricey, and not all of them offer financial aid — so ask.

Of course, you don't have to work with a specific program — many students teach English as part of a faith-based group, others travel with friends or family, and some work locally for a year. Whatever you end up planning can be great, as long as it's detailed, and made in advance with the help and support of parents and others who know you well.

Making a plan up as you go along usually spells disaster or lots of TV time on the couch, so if you're simply avoiding commitment, deferral probably isn't for you. Instead, you should put your jammies back on, grab one last handful of Cocoa Doodles, and look at the next chapter.

Chapter 53
STILL CAN'T DECIDE? TRY THIS.

If you're in need of some guidelines as you think your way to May 1st, try these:

- **Think college qualities, not college names.** There are reasons why you loved the colleges you applied to — the small class size, the classes they offer, the feel on campus. Write those qualities down, and see how each of your schools matches up to those qualities.

- **Visit the campuses — one way or another.** The last time you visited your colleges, you were thinking 'I guess this could work.' This isn't a time to guess — head back to campus with Mom and Dad, bring your list of qualities, and take a much closer look — including sitting in on classes if at all possible. If you can't get there (hey, time and money is tight), take the virtual tour on the college's Web site and see if the school is in *The Yale Insider's Guide* — that may bring back some memories, or show you some new things to consider.

- **De-brief at the end.** Once you're through remembering what you liked and didn't like, talk with your parents about what you saw. What qualities were on campus that you liked? What new questions do you have? Can you see yourself at this college?

- **Seek parental input.** It's great to show some independence, but your parents are the two people who know you best. Invite their expertise — "Mom, Dad, do you see me being happy here?"

- **Compare the colleges you have, not the ones you wanted.** Once you've toured the campuses, compare their strengths and weaknesses — but leave the dream school that denied you out of the picture. You might not find a perfect campus, but you'll most likely find a best one — focus on that goal, and you'll be fine.

- **Don't forget your heart.** You might not able to describe why a college is best for you, but that's OK. You've done a lot of research and thinking — at this point, you can trust your heart to lead you. Your head will remember why this college was best for you when you come to campus in the fall.

- **Think about what makes sense now.** When you applied to all of these places last Fall, you may have said, "If School X lets me in, I'm going there for sure." There's no doubt you felt that way last fall — but that was seven months ago, and your interests, passions, and way of looking at the world may be different now than they were then. How you felt then could be a factor, but it's a small one compared to how you feel now — keep that in mind.

- **Check finances one last time.** You still can't get two colleges in a bidding war over you, but if you have a college you love and it's a little out of reach, call the admissions and financial aid offices — that's usually two calls — and tell them so. A sincere call shows them you're interested; not calling at all gives them no impression at all — and may leave you short in the wallet for no reason at all.

- **Start the hunt again.** If your choices really don't thrill you, wait until May 5th. That's when colleges discover they have unexpected openings — and of course they'll want to fill them. Getting financial aid might be a challenge, but you never know — call the admissions office, or look at the Space Availability Report at *www.nacanet.org* — but remember, that may mean you risk having no school at all next fall.

Chapter 54

THE FINAL EXAM OF CHOOSING A COLLEGE

Now that you've narrowed your choices, there are just three questions left to consider:

Are you in love with what the college stands for, or with what that college has to offer you? Once a college admits you, they will call you day and night, send you e-mail hourly, and text you in the middle of math class. One college even went so far as to send each admitted student a disposable cell phone; that way, the college could be in touch all the time, since they already knew every student's phone number.

Some of this may be helpful — if a student calls who's majoring in your field, great — but many of these techniques are designed to create a feeling or glow about the college that can cloud your judgment, not clear it up. Same deal with financial aid packages; one student picked a school based on a $600 grant they'd given him, just because they called it an honors scholarship. That makes the school a little less expensive — but does it make it for you?

The college you say yes to will be thrilled to have you, and that's important — but you won't be getting hourly texts once you hit campus, or escorted to class by the school mascot every day. Classes, studying, peer relationships, and laundry will take up about 150 of your college days each year, while home football games will take up six. This is your new home — make sure the foundation of your choice of that home is solid.

Should you start locally and transfer? If money is tight, consider starting at a local community college or four-year school, living at home for a year or two, then transferring to your dream school. You'll have to work very closely with an adviser to make sure your classes will transfer, but if this means less loans, less stress, and more of a chance to afford your final two years at your dream school, it's worth considering.

It's May 1st, and you just can't decide which college to attend. Can you send deposits to more than one college? The answer is no. May 1st is the day you tell one college yes, and thank the others — but it's really only one, and it's really May 1st.

Consider this. You decide on a college that has small classes, which is perfect for you. You head to class the first day, only to find out that 30 students at this small college double deposited — on May 1st, they told your college they were coming, but also told another college they were coming. They all went to their other colleges, but didn't tell your college until yesterday. It's too late to offer those seats to other students, so what does your college do? Cancel classes, lay off teachers they can't afford to hire, and put students in classes of 100. So much for the education you had hoped for.

Telling lots of schools yes on May 1st is like saying yes to 10 prom dates — you get more time to choose, but it hurts everyone else, and in the end, someone else's indecision may hurt you. Students stay on waitlists for no reason, colleges schedule classes that won't have enough students, and parents lose deposits that could go for textbooks — or retirement.

It's great to have options, but the band is playing, and it's time to dance. Size up your partners, pick the one that will get you across the dance floor with the right balance of support and excitement, and move to the music of the future — your future.

Chapter 55

WHAT REALLY GOT YOU IN,
AND WHAT WILL REALLY KEEP YOU OUT

Now that you've decided on a college, you're probably engaged in serious academic pursuits, like planning senior skip day and sneaking a whoopee cushion on the principal's chair at graduation, so I'll quickly address two issues I have for you, and you can be on your way.

First, congratulations again on your acceptance into college. Your admission letter really is an affirmation of the hard work you put in, the risks you took in challenging yourself with tough classes, and the many contributions you made outside of the classroom.

I'm repeating this because many students often thank counselors or teachers for "getting them in" to college. I think I know what you mean when you say that, but I'm not sure you do.

Too many newspaper reporters try and make the college application process more "interesting" by shaping it like a reality TV show (*Survivor: Showdown on the Quad*). This explains why your parents gave you SAT flash cards for your first communion, or a gold bracelet for your bat mitzvah with the inscription *www.commonapp.org*. It also explains why your mother's therapist can send his daughter to Cornell without taking out any loans.

Thanks to the fourth estate, college counselors are viewed as the Dumbledores of College Access, the College Whisperers who bring you into their offices only to get a sense of your aura. Later, at a time when they sense the Force is with them, they call the college of your choice on a special red phone, whisper the Greek equivalent of "Baa Ram Ewe" into the mouthpiece, and *voila!* — you're admitted.

Of course, we make you jump through the hoops of earning good grades, getting up on several Saturdays to take tests where the correct answers always form a Scantron silhouette of Snoopy, and writing several drafts of college essays designed to get you to communicate your understanding of yourself and the world around you — but this is window dressing. The real work happens in our offices, when the moon is but a thin crescent in the southern sky and the wind blows towards Harvard Yard, Touchdown Jesus, or fraternity row at Faber College.

The world would have you believe this, but it isn't true. Yes, we help you find the right mix of challenge, support and opportunity at your next school. We also help you understand how to give colleges a complete picture of your life through the right mix of letters of recommendation, personal essays, and genuine interviews.

But we are not the ones who "get you in" — you earn the grades, write the essays, and make it happen. That's as it should be, since it is who you are and what you do that not only gets you into college; it keeps you there as well …

… which leads me to my second point. Colleges care about your last semester grades as much as the grades you earned in 9th grade — maybe a little more. It's great that you see college in sight, but if you slack off now, your decision to turn down the full ride scholarship to Daisy's Dog Grooming School will prove to have been a poor one.

If you need help remembering what it was you were studying before senioritis struck, you might want to track down Dumbledore and borrow his Pensieve. But remember, school counselors ain't Dumbledore — they honestly told the colleges you were a hard worker, and they'll have to honestly tell them you've stopped being so, if that's the case.

So, how about if you forget about the whoopee for now, and focus on the cushion?

Chapter 56

THINGS TO DO BEFORE COLLEGE

Graduates, here are some recommendations on how to spend your summertime. College is about trying new things, so give these a spin, and you'll hit the campus more flexible than Gumby after a yoga class:

Movie You Must See Before You Go To College: *The Shawshank Redemption* was overlooked when it was released the same year as *Forrest Gump.* Now it's on TNT every month. A story about second chances, forgiveness and negotiating with the world, this isn't an easy movie to watch, but it talk about hope, determination, and always knowing what's right. It will give you the skills to handle *Intro to Econ*, eccentric roommates, and more.

Movie Clip You Must See Before You Go to College: Call it cheesy, but the first scene in *The Sound of Music* is worth the five minutes and 46 seconds it will occupy in your life. All you see are the mountains of Austria, and all you hear is the remarkable voice of a young Julie Andrews. Success in college demands an ability to stop and appreciate that which is simple and beautiful. Watching this clip will also help you understand why your father's adolescence was complicated by having an intense crush on a nun.

Song You Must Listen to Before You Go To College: The second movement of Mozart's *Concerto for Flute and Harp* is the finest piece he ever wrote, and its potential was fully realized by Jean Pierre Rampal and Lily Laskine. Rampal started as a pre-med major, but his heart had other designs, and he went on to become the premiere flutist of all time. This reminds you that anyone who believes all works of Mozart are the same has no idea what listening is all about — keep that in mind. www.youtube.com/watch?v=k-UAsDV79eQ.

Song Clip You Must Watch Before You Go To College: It took less than two minutes for Ella Fitzgerald and the Manhattan Transfer to find their place in Grammy history in 1983 with this rendition of *How High the Moon.* Your goal in college is to work this hard to make everything look this easy — and if you leave college without an appreciation for good jazz, your tuition was wasted. *Http://www.youtube.com/watch?v=PBBiH92T-Ws&feature=realted.*

Phrases You Must Add to Your Vocabulary: "Ma'am" and "Sir." Colleges are run by administrative assistants — veteran, organized, professionals who have a way of doing things that is older than Stonehenge. This method almost always works to your advantage, except at peak times when every student needs help, and their system of order is on the brink of collapse. That's where you come in.

You: "I need to drop a class."

Administrative assistant, peering over half glasses: "Have you seen your adviser?"

You: "Yes sir/ma'am." *(Don't use both.)*

You have made their day, and he/she will never, ever, forget you.

This is good. Trust me.

Phrase You Must Delete from Your Vocabulary: "No problem." One of these assistants may thank you for doing something. The only way you can get off their good side is to respond with anything but, "You're Welcome." Practice now.

Book You Must Read Before You Go To College: *How the Irish Saved Civilization* by Thomas Cahill. Neither fiction nor a scholarly work, it's like your Irish neighbor telling you the enriched but true story of the vital role Irish monks held in restoring education to Europe during the time of St. Patrick. You won't read anything this easy or biased in college, but its story of how modest people can engage in diligent efforts that change history will stay with you forever.

Congratulations.

Chapter 57

ONCE YOU'RE THERE

Since you'll undoubtedly jump on social media to talk to your future roommate the minute you find out who they are, there's no point in saying make sure you figure out who's bringing the fridge (or if one's allowed); ditto for getting the early orientation dates, so you have ample classes to choose from.

The real challenge begins once you hit campus. What you do and choose not to do in the first two months is crucial to the rest of your freshman year, and to finishing college in general. If there's any chapter I hope you'll scan into your smart phone, it's this one and Chapter 58:

Set up a regular study routine. High school classes met every day; most of your college classes meet two or three times a week. The good news is that you now have free time Tuesday afternoons for the first time since you were five; the bad news is your time management skills for Tuesday afternoons haven't been tested in about 13 years.

The key is to set up a study schedule. Every college class is designed for you to complete two hours of note taking, studying, and re-reading for every hour you're in class, so block it in from Day 1. *Making College Count 2* offers some insights on how to make that work; some students find it a little too structured, but alter it to work to your liking, and develop a study plan more detailed than "later."

Don't study in your room. Studying in a library may be a new idea to you, but so is having all this free time — and there's a good chance some veteran geeks (or stern librarians) will show you the ropes. Try it for two weeks, and see what happens.

Get a real bank account. Unless you've had your own checking account (complete with debit card) for about five years, it's going to be way too easy to buy $5 coffee every day without seeing what that does to the same account you use to buy books. Make sure you get an account that's updated daily, and view it online at least three times a week

— you need to see what you're spending to understand what you can't afford.

Don't get a credit card. Offers to sign you up will be everywhere — at a table in the Student Union, in the bottom of your bookstore bag, and even at the stadium on the day of the big game. Trouble is, many of these offers are aimed at people who have little credit experience, who don't read the fine print — and if they do, there's so much of it, they can't sort out what it says anyway.

If you must have a credit card, talk with your parents about getting one before you get to campus. Chances are the terms will be friendlier, and the decision won't be hasty.

Volunteer in the community beyond the college. There's an active community around the campus, supporting the college students who use the town library, civic center, places of worship, and sometimes even parking meters, for free!

The townies do their fair share to keep things up, but you live there, too — so find the YMCA, elementary chess team, or wannabe Web designer club that could use your help, and pitch in. There's a part of you in that town that needs to be discovered, both by them, and by you — go find it.

Touch base with home at least weekly. Write, e-mail, teleconfer, phone, but it's a must.

Chapter 58

FOR SOMEDAY (I HOPE NOT)

Sometimes the life you build turns out to be the life you don't want to live after all. If that's where you are someday, I offer this story for you for safekeeping. I hope this lad's adventures do not await you — but in the event a day comes that leaves you wondering about your own capabilities, remember this.

My first client was a wreck. A bright enough boy, with good grades and test scores to boot — but no self-esteem. None. He clung to the sides of the hallway between classes, didn't ask many questions about college, and ended up in the honors college of a public university he had no business going to — for as nice a college as it was for some, he had other things to do, but he didn't know it.

Fall of the freshmen year came, and disaster was right at his heels. Between the blasting stereos and the late night screaming — and this was in the honors dorm — he finally figured out this wasn't the place for him. After two weeks, he packed his bags and headed for home. He managed to get into the fall semester of a nearby commuter college that started late, but he really longed for something different. He re-applied to another residential college, where he figured things might be better; he knew some students who went there, the campus was pretty, and it was big enough for him to be anonymous, just like always.

He headed out for his third college on New Year's Day, less than six months after he'd graduated from high school. After about three weeks, it was pretty clear this place wasn't heaven either, and yet something was different. The stereos weren't as loud — it was winter, after all — and a couple of the teachers talked to him like he was a human being, so he decided this was the place to make his stand. For once, he was going to steer his destiny, and not the other way around.

With that change in attitude, things worked out pretty well. He met up with some high school friends, who invited him to join their intramural basketball and softball teams (he was awful, but it didn't matter all that much — so were they). His understanding of classical music impressed a couple of girls enough to get past his low self-esteem and go out on a couple of dates — nothing intense, but certainly reassuring. His academic interests led him to work as an assistant on a research project studying language development among American children — groundbreaking stuff at the time — and he gained the respect of many of his instructors, especially the writing profs, who told him he really had something, if he wanted to work at it.

Twenty-four months after he started at his third college — two and a half years after graduating from high school — he signed his first employment contract. Two days after that, he walked across the commencement stage, not once, but twice, having earned enough credits for two separate degrees, making him the first member of his family to graduate from college, and a working stiff to boot.

Three months after that, he turned 20.

I know you have worked very hard to build the very best future you possibly can. In the event your current plan should go awry, there will be another plan for another day — listen closely, always be receptive to the possible, and know that the choice to succeed is ultimately yours, and yours alone … but you will never be alone.

Chapter 59
WHAT'S NEXT

I said this book wouldn't be perfect, and I'm sorry to say I was right. We didn't get to a lot of things, but I think we covered enough of the ground rules to give you the big picture. Most people think getting into a good college is about rocket science or tea leaves, when it's really about hard work, focus, curiosity, and knowing what it means to take a deep, full breath. Colleges want to know what you've done in the world so far, and what you think your role in the world of tomorrow might be. If you can get that into an application, you'll get into any college that's great for you, and you'll have everything you need to live (one more time!) a rich, full life.

As promised, I won't leave you hanging in the wind, unless that's where you choose to be. Your next step is to visit www.collegeisyours.com to join the discussion with other college seekers and ask your questions. Applying to college always changes from year to year, and others can benefit from what you have to say — so come on over and tell us what you know, and others will do the same.

Two more things before class is dismissed. First, you have a pretty good clue about how to choose a college; now, you have to put it in practice. It doesn't matter where you go, when you go, how many you go to, or if you don't go at all — you've got enough here to build a future on something other than hope, what your friends are doing about life, or "beats me." Run if you want to — you read the book, and it's too late to pretend you're stupid. Take a breath, catch a dream, and ride it wherever it will take you; you have the skills to hang on, hang in, and hold your head high, because knowledge is freedom …

… the freedom to choose among wise options. As you celebrate senior year, getting into college, and graduation, there's a good chance you'll be hanging out at parties and celebrations that are pretty wide open. This is especially true at college, where there will be no bells to remind you about what to do or when to do it, which means the choices are pretty much up to you.

I don't want this to turn into a Health class lecture, or (even worse) a Political Science lecture about the necessity of law; instead, let me tell remind you of some ideas you probably already know:

- Developmentally, you aren't through growing yet, and the fine tuning your body is doing now requires as few pollutants as possible. In addition, many of you may still be in a developmental phase where the use of drugs and alcohol now could create a dependency that will be difficult to shake, not just now, but ever — so yes, 20 is different from 21.

- The later it gets, the better the chance the guy driving next to you is drunk. It's an old statistic, but I once read that one out of every three cars on the road after 11pm on the weekend — one out of every three — is being driven by a legally drunk driver.

- Legally, drunk driving, possession of alcohol by a minor, furnishing alcohol to a minor, and possession and sale of illegal drugs to anyone are crimes. If convicted, this information can be devastating to a college application, as well as applications for loans, employment, military service — and lives beyond just yours.

As a counselor, part of my job is to help you create the best future you can possibly have; to that end, from now until forever, do the following:

- Do not, under any circumstance, get in a car driven by a drunk driver (any drunk driver), or in a car where alcohol or drugs are being used. Both are unsafe; with the latter, you'll go to jail, and with the former, you could end up hurt, or worse.

- If you're driving after 11 pm, plan a route home that gets you past the fewest number of bars and restaurants as possible.

- If offered a substance that is unsafe, unwise, or illegal for you to use, graciously say no. If being gracious is impossible, you have someplace better to be, and truer friends to be with — pull out your car keys, or make that call, and move on.

Blind obedience to stupid laws is questionable — I think life teaches us all that. However, obedience to a law you may not fully understand is a different thing. You've worked hard to build a bright future- do yourself and the world a favor, stick around to live it out, and I promise you that one day the law you might not fully understand will make stone cold sober perfect sense ...

... and if you think I'm saying that just because it's my job, let me point out this is the longest chapter in the book, by far.

I guess I'm busted.

Don't you be.

Chapter 60
600 WORDS FOR PARENTS

Dudes and dudettes, this bit is just for the folks.

Really.

So go already!

* * * * *

Thank you for the interest you're taking in your child's life, and in their college choice. I'd like to think I know the college selection process well, but you're a clear expert about your child (hopefully, second only to them). With the right balance of ideas and participation from you and me, your son or daughter will have the best possible foundation to build a great college choice on.

I have a couple of suggestions to make this process work well for you. First, you really do need to see yourself as an expert. You might not know everything about your child, but your willingness to use what you know and let them teach you more will make a huge difference, before, during, and after college.

Second, you need to see this process in a way that makes sense to you. If you've never had a child choose a college, or if it's been a while, you'll see it's very different than when you chose a college — there's more information, more preparation, and more choice. It's like the difference between buying a house in a buyer's market or a seller's market — the product is the same, but the rules are very different.

As you read this book and work with your child, I hope you'll use your house/apartment hunting experience as a model. Like house hunting, it's great to see pictures, do Internet research, and run spreadsheets on colleges — but the way you know a house will really work is to see it, feel it, and take it in. You don't always (or ever) find the perfect house, but you start with a list of what it has to have, go out looking, maybe change the list a little, find a few that will work — and a first choice emerges. After doing more research, running a cost analysis, lining up financing, and just letting things sink in, you put in an offer, and see how it lines up with that of other bidders. If it all works out, you're in; if not, you've got another house that will be just as nice, only in a different way.

In a nutshell, that's the college selection process — just don't try to explain it that way to teenagers, since their experience in house buying is a little slim.

Third, do everything you can to let your children own this experience. Your athletic daughter didn't make the select travel team by letting you try out, and your son the all-state oboe player didn't make the audition by having you practice for him. As with all things, your emotional and logistical support is vital to this process — but be careful to let them lead. Chapter 11 talks about *the* tried and true way to maintain a good balance of your interest and their independence. Start at the beginning of the book, then enjoy that chapter when it comes up — unless you're already planning to fill out the college applications for your child, in which case you should read that chapter now, and develop Plan B for the applications.

Parents of college bound students often say fear, a lack of knowledge, or love for their child is what motivates them in helping their children find a college. In 25 years of doing this, I can tell you the only successful, supportive relationships in the college selection process are the ones built on love. Let that be the one and only motive behind all you do, and all will go well.

About the Author

Patrick O'Connor is on the Political Science Faculty of Oakland Community College and is Director of College Counseling at The Roeper School, both in Metropolitan Detroit. Born and raised in Detroit, he has been a college counselor since 1984, serving students in rural, urban, and suburban high schools, as well as community college. In addition to writing a weekly column at www.collegeisyours.com, his writing has appeared in High School Counselor Week, MyFootpath.com, The Christian Science Monitor, The Washington Post, The Detroit Free Press and Diverse: Issues in Higher Education.

Patrick has served as president of the Michigan Association for College Admission Counseling, and the National Association for College Admission Counseling. He is on the Board of Directors of the Michigan College Access Network, and on the credentialing commission for the American Institute of Certified Educational Planners. He is a recipient of the Outstanding Faculty Award from Oakland Community College, the Margaret Addis Service to NACAC Award, and the William Gramenz Award (for outstanding contributions to college counseling in Michigan). He holds five college degrees, including a Ph.D. in Education Administration.

Patrick lives with his wife and children in suburban Detroit, and can be reached at collegeisyours@comcast.net.